# A Treatise On Isometrical Drawing As Applicable to Geological and Mining Plans

CAPHEATON,

1668.

# A

## TREATISE

### ON

# ISOMETRICAL DRAWING

### BY

## T. SOPWITH.

CHESTERHOLME.

A

# TREATISE

ON

# ISOMETRICAL DRAWING,

AS APPLICABLE TO

## GEOLOGICAL AND MINING PLANS,

PICTURESQUE DELINEATIONS OF

### Ornamental Grounds,

PERSPECTIVE VIEWS AND WORKING PLANS OF

## BUILDINGS AND MACHINERY,

AND TO GENERAL PURPOSES OF

### Civil Engineering;

WITH DETAILS OF IMPROVED METHODS OF PRESERVING
PLANS AND RECORDS OF SUBTERRANEAN OPERATIONS
IN MINING DISTRICTS.

WITH THIRTY-FOUR COPPERPLATE ENGRAVINGS.

### BY T. SOPWITH,

LAND AND MINE SURVEYOR,

MEMBER OF THE INSTITUTION OF CIVIL ENGINEERS,
AUTHOR OF "GEOLOGICAL SECTIONS OF MINES,"
"ACCOUNT OF MINING DISTRICTS," &c.

"Isometrical perspective is preferable to common perspective on many accounts ;
it is much easier and simpler in its principles ; it is also incomparably more easy
and accurate in its application. The information given by isometrical drawings
is much more definite and precise than that obtained by the usual methods, and
better fitted to direct a workman in execution."     PROFESSOR FARISH.

"Isometrical views of buildings ought to be in universal use among architects."
"The elevation which this mode of drawing produces, is highly explanatory and
expressive."                                             J. C. LOUDON.

### London:

JOHN WEALD,
TAYLOR'S ARCHITECTURAL LIBRARY,

59, HIGH HOLBORN.

1834.

# PREFACE.

THE object of this work is, to elucidate the
principles of Isometrical Projection, and to explain its application to a variety of useful purposes.

In the construction of Geological Maps, and
of Plans and Sections of Mines, Isometrical
Drawing produces a clear and interesting delineation of the various strata, and combines many
peculiar advantages which cannot be obtained
by any other method.

As this subject is one which is daily increasing
in interest, and as the necessity of preserving
accurate plans and records of mines is now generally appreciated, the Author has included
several observations on this department of engineering, and has also given many practical details

connected with the surveying and planning of mines, which he trusts will be found useful to those who are studying the profession. These details are the result of considerable experience, which the Author has had in various extensive surveys of mining districts, and of frequent opportunities of deriving information from many Owners and Agents of Mines, to whom he has submitted his suggestions, and been favoured with a liberal and friendly expression of their opinions respecting them.

For Plans and Elevations of Buildings, and for working details of Machinery, Isometrical Drawing possesses such decided advantages, that a more extended knowledge of its principles cannot fail to ensure its almost universal application, in preference to every other mode of perspective drawing.

In representing Gardens and Pleasure Grounds, not only a correct plan of the mansion, and the various walks, lawns, or plantations, can be shown, but also the height and pictorial aspect of the trees, shrubs, green-houses, &c. For this and various other purposes, Isometrical Drawing will be found an agreeable occupation to Amateur Artists, and especially to Ladies, who are thus enabled to combine the beauties of Landscape, Architectural, and Flower Painting, with useful and correct delineations of pleasure grounds, houses, gardens, or other objects.

To the above, and to drawings of Harbours, Bridges, and other engineering Plans, the application of this almost unknown, but extremely beautiful and simple, mode of projection is explained. The especial object of the Author is to furnish a book which may be practically useful and intelligible to every class of readers : and geometrical illustrations are also introduced for the information of mathematical students, for which the Author is indebted to the eminent talents of his respected friend, Mr. Peter Nicholson, the well-known author of many valuable works in various departments of Architecture and Geometry.

Brief as the work is, it has been much delayed by the urgency of various Plans and Surveys, and

by frequent absence in London and Gloucester-
shire.    Those who are at all acquainted with the
correction of the press, and the comparing of
simultaneous letter-press and copperplate engravings, will readily appreciate this inconvenience ; and any discrepancies (which, however,
the Author hopes are both few and unimportant,)
are thus accounted for, and will, he trusts, have
the favourable indulgence of his readers.

# CONTENTS.*

---

## CHAPTER I.

### ON MINERAL PLANS AND SURVEYS.

* The great number and interest of the publications of the present day
render it desirable that every facility of reference should be given by a
condensed synopsis of contents, &c. This ought to be more especially observed in books of a practical and scientific nature, for the time of most of
the readers of such works is too fully occupied by their respective avocations
to admit of their wading through a terra incognita of reading in search of
particular points of information. For want of such references, many valuable suggestions on matters of art and science, as well as many useful practical details, remain comparatively unknown; and no apology, it is trusted,
is necessary for the copious Table of Contents, Explanation of Plates, &c., in
this volume, as an attentive study of the subject may require frequent reference as well to the plates as to different portions of the treatise.

## CHAPTER II.

### ISOMETRICAL PROJECTION.

## PROPOSITIONS.

* The substance of this portion of the work was given in a verbal explanation to the Institution of Civil Engineers in May, 1833, when the Author also exhibited the use of the triangular rulers for projecting isometrical drawings. It may be proper to mention that 128 pages of this work were printed when the Author received the first number of Mr. Jopling's work called the Practice of Isometrical Perspective, which will be found a useful aid to all who are desirous of being fully acquainted with this mode of drawing. It forms a neat 8vo. vol., price four shillings, and contains a great number of diagrams illustrative of isometrical projection.

† Among the numerous scientific and intelligent persons who have been pleased to express a favourable opinion of this example of the application of isometrical drawing to geological plans, I am gratified to perceive that so acute and experienced a critic as Mr. Loudon has made favourable mention of it in one of his publications.

‡ For a familiar illustration of these definitions, with references to Figs 4 in Plates VIII. and IX., see p. 133.

* This further illustration of the subject is introduced as a guide to mathematical instrument makers, to whom the Author is willing to afford any information respecting this or any other instruments applicable to isometrical drawing. The projecting rulers shown in Plate XVI. are sold at a moderate price, and are extremely useful for many purposes, as well as for isometrical drawing.

## CHAPTER III.

### ISOMETRICAL DRAWING.

[*] It is by means of this distinction, or by the proportional enlargement of
the isometrical plan or drawing, as compared with a strict isometrical projection, that the same scale which is used for any common ground elevation
or section, &c., becomes applicable to the isometrical plan or drawing of the
same object.

## CHAPTER IV.

### APPLICATION OF ISOMETRICAL DRAWING TO GEOLOGY AND MINING.

## CHAPTER V.

### APPLICATION OF ISOMETRICAL DRAWING TO ORNAMENTAL AND LANDSCAPE GARDENING.

b*

## CHAPTER VI.

### APPLICATION OF ISOMETRICAL DRAWING TO PLANS OF BUILDINGS AND MACHINERY, AND TO GENERAL PURPOSES OF CIVIL ENGINEERING.

# EXPLANATION OF THE PLATES.

WITH A REFERENCE TO THE SEVERAL PAGES IN WHICH THEY
ARE RESPECTIVELY DESCRIBED.

### FRONTISPIECE.

CAPHEATON HALL, Northumberland, the seat of Sir John
Swinburne, Bart., Page 202.

#### TITLE PAGE VIGNETTE.

CHESTERHOLME, Northumberland, the residence of the Rev. A.
Hedley, Page 207.

##### PLATE I. MINERAL PLANS.

Form for preserving plans of mines, with titles, scales, and references in a side column, regularly numbered and bound in volumes.
Part of a series of mineral plans, made from actual survey by the
Author, for His Majesty's Commissioners of Woods and Forests, is
preserved in this form, which is much more convenient for reference
than large and unwieldy plans. Pages 18, 19, 42, 173.

##### PLATE II. COMPARATIVE SCALES FOR PLANS OF LAND, ROADS, OR MINES.

A square acre of land, with roads, house, plantation, shaft, &c., is
delineated on this plate respectively to 1, 2, 3, 4, 5, 6, 8, 10, 20, 40,
80, and 160 chains to an inch, in order to show the relative size of

these several objects to different scales. The squares marked, Fig. 3, represent areas of one square acre of subterranean workings as practised in the mines of the Newcastle coal district. (In the description, page 21, by an error of the press, the pillars are called 8 yards square, for which read 8 yards by 20.)

### PLATE III. SILVER BAND MINE.

This engraving is reduced one-fourth from an engraved plan and section made for the company agreeably to the proposal in page 47. Pages 23, 37, 50, 167. The original formed one of the geological sections of mines published by the Author in 1828, and the copperplate was subsequently transmitted to Robert Surtees, Esq., of Mainsforth, who purposed inserting it as an illustration of the geology of Teesdale, in his History of Durham. A note from Mr. Surtees relative to this plate in Feb. 1834, was the last communication which the Author had with this much-esteemed friend and patron, whose valuable life and labours were terminated, after a few days' illness, on the 11th of the same month, to the most unfeigned sorrow of all who admired his splendid talents, and still more estimable virtues.

### PLATE IV. SHAFTOE ESTATE.

This plan contains nearly a thousand acres of land, plotted to a scale of 32 chains to an inch, or 2½ in. to a mile. The strong lines indicate the boundaries of each farm, and the shading represents the bold and picturesque eminence, called Shaftoe Crags. This and the following Plate are introduced as specimens of a convenient form for preserving plans of estates and farms, and also as exemplifying the clearness and accuracy which may be combined in a very small scale. Page 25.

### PLATE V. SHAFTOE FARM.

This is a portion of the preceding plan enlarged to a scale of 16 chains to an inch, or 5 inches to a mile. Plans of this kind may be reduced from existing plans at a very moderate expense, and when carefully drawn, and neatly coloured, form a collection no less useful as a book of constant reference at the escrutoir of a nobleman or gentleman, than as an occasional companion for proprietors or agents in riding over the estates thus represented in a portable and explanatory form. Page 25.

### PLATE VI. HUDGILL CROSS VEIN.

This plate represents part of the subterranean workings of a lead mine in the manor of Alston Moor, and the representation of strata veins, adits, &c., is strictly limited to these respective objects as actually measured. See pages 36, 51, 152.

### PLATE VII. COAL AND LEAD WORKINGS.

Fig. 1 is given as an example of representing coal workings, and is a small part of one of the collieries of David Mushet, Esq., in the Forest of Dean. The double lines represent the deep levels and air courses, and the parts where coal has been excavated are shown by shaded lines, the small letters and figures being references to a descriptive report and explanations which accompany the mineral plans and sections of the mines in that district, made by the Author for His Majesty's Commissioners of Woods and Forests, &c. Fig. 2 represents a portion of Holyfield Lead Mine, in the manor of Alston Moor. The section exhibits the several adits, rises, &c., and the plan shows the horizontal portion of the same. The shading indicates not only the position of the mineral workings, but also the comparative richness of the veins, as described in page 40.

### PLATE VIII. ISOMETRICAL CUBE.

The diagrams on this plate very clearly exhibit the general principles of isometrical projection, and also the distinction between the true *isometrical projection* of a cube, and the enlarged *isometrical drawing* which extends the edges to the same length as the square above, when measured by a common scale. Pages 124, 126.

### PLATE IX. ISOMETRICAL VIEW AND SECTIONS.

The ground plan and two sections, which are all united on one isometrical drawing, afford a simple but very explanatory idea of isometrical drawing, which consists in applying the same principles of representation to various objects, however irregular in shape. See pages 70, 128.

### PLATE X. ISOMETRICAL PROJECTION.

The diagrams in this plate, with the corresponding propositions in Chapter II., elucidate the mathematical principles of isometrical projection and drawing. The following are the references to the respective explanations:—Fig. 1, page 81. Fig. 2, page 82. Fig. 3, page 83. Fig. 4, page 84. Fig. 5, page 85. Fig. 6, page 86. Fig. 7, page 86.

### PLATE XI. ISOMETRICAL PROTRACTOR.

Fig. 1 is the diagonal triangle on which depend the dimensions of the isometrical ellipse in Fig. 2, see page 87. The construction of the protractor is minutely detailed in page 97, and sequel, and the practical details are further elucidated by a diagram in Plate XV.

### PLATE XII. PERSPECTIVE AND PROJECTION.

The nature of projection and perspective is clearly exemplified in the several diagrams of this plate, and the able demonstrations of the subject by Mr. Nicholson, in page 88, and sequel.

### PLATE XIII. ISOMETRICAL PLANS OF LAND.

These diagrams are given as examples of the easy and expeditious manner in which the lengths and bearings, or angles, of any survey may be plotted on an isometrical plan. Page 104.

### PLATE XIV. ISOMETRICAL PLANS OF HOUSES.

The delineation of a house or other architectural object, in any position, is explained by two examples, one having a south aspect, the other an aspect to the south declining to the west 70°. Pages 108, 111.

### PLATE XV. ISOMETRICAL ELLIPSE.

Diagrams illustrative of the construction of ellipses and of the isometrical protractor. Pages 97, 113.

### PLATE XVI. PROJECTING AND PARALLEL RULERS.

These rulers may be made sufficiently correct for most practical purposes by pasting the engraving upon thin mahogany or plaintree, and planing the edges very carefully to the border lines or scale of each triangle, the space between being left for a saw cut; but ivory rules, with fiducial edges, would be neater and more accurate.— For the description and use, see page 137.

### PLATE XVII. ISOMETRICAL DRAWING,

Contains several examples of the use of the projecting and parallel rulers, and a representation of Professor Farish's isometrical T square, or bevel. Pages 135, 142.

### PLATE XVIII. GEOLOGICAL MODEL.

This plate illustrates the remarks on the construction of geological models, page 155, and the isometrical representation of a series of sections, as described in page 157.

### PLATE XIX. ISOMETRICAL LANDSCAPE.

The section, Fig. 1, is constructed from bearings and dimensions, the process of which is detailed in pages 104, 159, 162, and 163; the delineation of Fig. 2 is described in pages 104.

### PLATE XXVII. TANFIELD ARCH.

This arch, which is 103 feet span, was thrown over a deep and romantic valley near Newcastle, by the partnership of colliery owners called " the Grand Allies," for the express purpose of conveying coals from the pits to the river Tyne. It has been long disused, and is falling rapidly to decay. This representation exhibits the walls, &c., restored, and the example was selected as possessing some interest as a picturesque object in a romantic valley, and at the same time a suitable illustration of the adaptation of isometrical drawing to works of this description. Page 232.

### PLATE XXVIII. CIRCULAR CAST IRON FRAMING.

Fig. 1 is a plan, Fig. 2 an elevation, and Fig. 3 an isometrical drawing, of one of the very ingenious cast iron structures invented by Mr. Davison, Engineer, of Truman's Brewery, London, for supporting the immense circular tuns of that establishment. The economy of material, and the lightness and simplicity of the design, have been much admired, and evince a union of practical knowledge with great taste in effecting so judicious a combination of strength and ornament. Page 233.

### PLATE XXIX. SEAHAM HARBOUR.

The upper part of this plate is a fac-simile of an engraved plan of Mr. Chapman's design for Seaham Harbour, and under it is an isometrical representation of the same, in which, for the sake of clearness, the principal lines of piers, &c., only are introduced. Page 234.

### PLATE XXX. MISCELLANEOUS.

Church Tower, Page 217. Monument, Page 219. Wheel, Page 220. Arch in an in-isometrical plane, page 229.

### PLATE XXXI. NEW DROP FOR SHIPPING COALS.

Plan, elevation, and section of a design by the late William Chapman, Esq. Page 234.

### PLATE XXXII. ISOMETRICAL DRAWING OF NEW DROP FOR SHIPPING COALS.

This representation, though necessarily on a small scale, exhibits the effect of isometrical drawings of machinery, &c., which possess all the boldness of perspective, though drawn by rules incomparably more easily understood, and more rapidly executed. Page 234.

# INDEX

## OF

# TECHNICAL TERMS.

-------

Many of the technical terms used in the present work being alto-gether new, and as frequent repetitions of them occur in elucidating the several subjects of the treatise. the following references are given in order that the reader may easily refer to the explanation of the respective terms. Some other references are also given, which may be useful or explanatory to the general reader.

* For drawing isometrical ellipses, the following index to those contained in the Plates of this work may be useful, as, by means of tracing paper, they may be easily transferred, so as to represent a circle or wheel of corresponding diameter

C *

---

The term ISOMETRICAL is derived from the Greek ἴσος, *equal*,
and μέτρον, *measure*.

# CHAPTER I.

## ON MINERAL PLANS AND SURVEYS.

THE great expense attendant on mining operations, the strict geometrical accuracy required in
projecting and conducting them, the difficulty of
access which militates against a frequent and
close inspection of the interior of mines, and the
decay which, on their abandonment, so speedily
renders them altogether inaccessible, are circumstances which strongly evince the great importance of having clear and accurate delineations
of the several works connected with them. To
lead mines these remarks are particularly applicable; for in them workings which have been
long abandoned frequently become the objects of
fresh adventure, and a needless repetition of labour and expense is often incurred by ignorance
of what has formerly been done. That minute
and faithful records of all subterranean works in

A

important mining districts have not been carefully preserved, is a matter of regret to all who are practically acquainted with the nature and utility of such documents.   On this subject, the eloquent declamation of Werner cannot be too often repeated, nor too earnestly pressed on the attention of all who are interested in the welfare of mining, or in the promotion of geological science. After describing the manner in which mining plans should be constructed, and commenting on the advantages of having such plans, and also geognostic descriptions of every mining district, he observes,—" Such a collection, the plan and description of the district, form together a complete and instructive whole.   If our ancestors had left us such documents for two centuries past, or even for half a century, what advantage would it not have been to us ?   From what doubts would it not relieve us ?   With what anxiety do we not turn over the leaves of ancient chronicles in search of information, often very imperfect, obscure, and uncertain ?   With what pleasure do we not receive the least sketch or plan of some ancient mine?   With what pains do we not rake up the old heaps of rubbish brought out of old excavations, to discover pieces which may afford us some idea of the substances which were formerly worked

out? Yet, between these documents, and
those which we might obtain in the way pointed out in the preceding paragraphs, there is as
much difference as between night and day. Is
it not an obligation, a duty, for us to collect
and leave to future generations as much instruction and knowledge as possible on the
labours carried on in our mines, whether it be
in those that are still worked, or in those which
have been given up?"

Such was the opinion of this eminent geologist,
whose knowledge of practical mining adds great
weight to the recommendation. He notices the
historical interest and scientific instruction afforded by such records, and not only in these respects, but as regards the actual profit and loss
of mining adventure, his well-merited encomiums
are borne out by the testimony of the most experienced geologists and miners. The publication
of Werner's directions for constructing plans, and
preserving geognostic descriptions of mineral districts, together with other similar works, diffused
much useful information on the subject, and led
to a more general adoption of plans in conducting
subterranean works; but the progress of improvement in this department of science has been slow,
and Werner's recommendation far from being universally, or even generally, attended to.

The utility of recording subterranean operations has been much undervalued by persons unacquainted with mining details, as well as by many of the less-informed class of mining adventurers, who are with difficulty brought to perceive the advantages, or to adopt the practice, of any system to which they have been unaccustomed: hence the plans of mines in this country are generally confined to such particulars only as are indispensable for conducting the subterranean works, without any reference to the past history and future prospects of the mine, or any sufficient record of the strata and various geological features. The accumulation of such a mass of practical information would in time prove of incalculable benefit, and eventually obtain that consideration to which it is so much entitled.

So long as an indifference to the general advancement of geology, in connection with mining, prevails, it is in vain to expect that any material improvement can be effected in planning subterranean works; but the progress of science, and the efforts of intelligent practical miners, seem likely to open out a wide field of observation and enquiry, and to pave the way for a more general and scientific system of recording the progress of mineral works in the great coal and lead-mining districts of the United Kingdom.

In a work professing to offer practical details concerning improved methods of constructing geological and mining plans, it is desirable, in the first place, to point out some of those considerations which render plans and sections so important in the economy of practical mining; and also to advert to the increasing necessity which exists for a more rigid attention being paid to such documents, than has hitherto been commonly bestowed upon them.

Subterranean wealth differs from other property chiefly in the extreme uncertainty of its existence, and the difficulty of its discovery. The valuable mining manor of Alston Moor was, upwards of 200 years ago, considered to be nearly exhausted of. its mineral treasures, though it abounded in those hidden and almost boundless stores, which have since been so fruitful a source of employment and opulence. A few scanty hints relative to the history of mining in Alston Moor extend to a period of nearly six hundred years ago ; but, excepting some information on the royal charters and privileges granted to the miners, no records remain to perpetuate the works connected with it. The situation and extent of the various mines which have, from century to century, been prosecuted, might have been clearly delineated and preserved at an expense exceedingly small in comparison with the expenditure of mining, and would have proved of incalculable value in promoting the interests of mining and the advancement or geological science.   Not only ought such records to consist of mere plans and sections, but should be accompanied with explanations of the reasons why they were forsaken, in what state the several workings were left, and whether there remained in them any inducements for the expenditure of capital in further adventures.   Of late years, the subject has received a considerable share of attention; but much remains to be done before any permanent and scientific record of mining operations can be generally adopted, on a scale commensurate with the importance and utility of the undertaking.

Among other causes which have retarded the progress of improvement in mineral plans and sections, as well as other regular details of subterranean operations, the speculative and uncertain nature of mining is one of the principal. Lead mining, in particular, has been viewed so much as a mere lottery, as to induce a neglect of those regular accounts and other records which are found so indispensable in other transactions. But mining, though certainly speculative, is not

entirely the work of chance: in it, as in all
other business, he who classifies his accounts,
and can at any time readily ascertain the exact
sources of expenditure and income, who derives
experience from the constant accumulation of
facts, and can comprehend the whole extent and
object of subterranean works, possesses very superior advantages over those who have no such
data. The well-founded calculations of the one
are, in the ordinary course of affairs, much more
likely to be attended with success than the vague
and unsatisfactory speculations of the other, who
(and experience daily testifies the fact) are often
involved in difficulties that might have been easily
avoided, and in expenses which need never to
have been incurred.

A reliance on *chance*, instead of science, as the
presiding genius of mining adventure, must, sooner
or later, affect its own existence, by demonstrating
that the singular instances of good fortune which
sometimes occur, bear a very small proportion
to the numerous undertakings which, begun
and continued without any means of appreciating
the employment of capital, and the condition of
the works, end in disappointment, and create a
highly-injurious prejudice against mining speculations. This prevailing idea of the uncertainty
of mining adventures, and a consequent disregard

of method in conducting them, are especially detrimental to the interests of such districts as mainly depend on private adventure for the discovery of the mineral treasures they contain. The *prospects* of mining cannot, indeed, be reduced to certainty, but it is exceedingly desirable *that all the details of conducting it* should be so. An intelligent system of this kind would attach to it a character of skill and method, for want of which it is much undervalued as a means of employing capital, and an opening has been thus afforded to impositions which have greatly lessened the public confidence in such undertakings. Whatever tends to increase a knowledge of mining undoubtedly contributes to its permanent interests; and if the present depression of the markets continue, if prices will not rise to meet the present and increasing expenditure of mines, there is the greater necessity for the adoption of every means to promote future economy, and to prevent future waste.

A residence of some years in the lead mining districts, with considerable practice in mineral surveying and planning, and repeated conversations with many intelligent proprietors and agents of mines, led me, a few years ago, to form those opinions of the value of, and increasing necessity for, accurate mining records; and they have since been further confirmed by subsequent enquiry, and by

the judgment of those who, by a practical knowledge, added to long experience of mining, are
best able to.form a correct opinion on the subject.

Since the production of the first geological
maps, by the Board of Agriculture, in 1794, the
progress of geology, as a science, has advanced
such maps to a considerable degree of perfection.
The transactions of various societies, and the
publication of numerous plans and sections, have
furnished many admirable examples of the interesting and beautiful manner in which the complicated
details of geological structure can be rendered intelligible.    This excellence, however, has not yet
extended to mining plans, at least to any considerable extent.    Most of these consist merely of
outlines of the course of the principal workings,
without any delineation of the several strata, or of
the relative productiveness of the works at different
periods.    Sectional plans, which are of great utility,
are far from being general; and I know of one
establishment only in which a regular series of them
is preserved.    A great source of imperfection in
such plans is, the want of an uniform and practical
mode of reducing the inequalities of hilly ground
to a plain surface.    Rules for doing this are learned
by almost every school-boy, but either a difference
in the practical method of ascertaining and repre-

senting these inequalities, or a total disregard of them, is the frequent source of very material errors.

Among other causes which contribute to the imperfect state of mining plans may be mentioned the want of a popular treatise on the subject, which should familiarly explain the mode of using different surveying and drawing instruments, illustrate the principles of representing horizontal, vertical, and inclined planes, and point out the best way of taking the measurements required for each. Examples should be given of the best methods of representing the different parts of mines, and an attempt be made to fix on general characters for that purpose. For want of such information, many miners, who can dial with accuracy, are at a loss how to represent on paper what they have measured; and some fruitlessly attempt to lay down and connect horizontal and vertical objects on one orthographic plane. What on one plan represents an adit, on another represents a vein or dyke; and such plans, therefore, for want of uniform modes of representing similar objects, can never be of any general or permanent utility. That these and many other imperfections exist to a considerable extent, is well known to those conversant with the subject, and they are here alluded to as forming some apology for an attempt to propose any amendments.

For the preservation of records of subterranean works, a strictly accurate plan of the district in which they are situated is essential. Owing to several causes, plans of mountainous counties have not in general been constructed with that extreme regard to accuracy, without which any inference as regards either geology or mining must be fallacious. The want of system in reducing hills to a plain surface, the uncertain weather and boisterous climate of such districts, so unfavourable to the use of good instruments, and the neglect of a very strict and indispensable regard to the variation of the magnetic needle, have all tended to occasion a great want of accuracy in plans of mines and of mineral districts.

In these introductory remarks, it is proposed to offer a few practical suggestions on the subject of geological and mining plans. Some of these have chiefly a reference to the lead mining districts; and it may be observed, that in them a greater necessity for improvement exists than in the coal mines. The proprietors of lead mines, in those districts which are open to public speculation, are a much more numerous body than the coal-owners; and, from the comparative smallness of their shares, cannot take that immediate interest in them which is absolutely requisite in large collieries. The value of lead and copper ores, and the cost of their production, are so variable, that veins which at one time will not pay the expense of working, will at another amply recompense the adventurer; and hence the greater necessity for preserving a faithful record of the condition and relative value of every vein. Coal mines require close and constant inspection, and the several galleries of communication are usually kept under careful regulation until finally abandoned; while the workings of lead mines are often abandoned for a period, suffered to decay, and again opened out for fresh trials. The viewers of coal mines usually keep regular working plans of the various workings, but, except in one instance, already alluded to, I have never met with any regularly-continued sectional plans of lead mines, though the utility of them is manifest to those who are well acquainted with the nature and prospects of mining. As it is from this consideration that the present work is undertaken, and from which it must derive its chief utility, it may be desirable, in addition to the opinion of Werner already quoted, to add the following testimonies from authorities whose evidence is the best confirmation of what is here advanced on the subject. Concerning the lead mines, Mr. Taylor, of London, an eminent engineer, extensively engaged in mining, observes, in a report concerning the extensive mineral district of Alston moor, which is placed under his superintendence,—

" One thing I think of great importance, which is, that PERFECT RECORDS of what has been done in the pursuit of every vein on the estate should be preserved; and I would recommend, for this purpose, that in all future leases a clause should be introduced, to require the adventurers to keep SECTIONS and PLANS of all their workings; and that the officers of the hospital should have power to inspect and copy them at all times; and it would follow, of course, that the moor master, or some competent person, should delineate these on a general plan, and preserve a collection of the sections of each mine."

As regards the coal mining district, the following remarks, by Mr. Buddle, are equally conclusive as to the necessity which exists for improved -methods of preserving subterranean records.

" It is obvious that many collieries which are now open will sooner or later be shut up, and lie dormant for various and indefinite periods—and the probability is, that in many cases all knowledge of the dykes which intersect them may be lost, and that the parties having to re-open them may be as ignorant, or even more so, than those who first opened these mines.

" It is not necessary that I should dwell on the extent of the loss of property and of lives which may result from such a state of things. My object is to draw the attention of the society,* and of the public to the means of avoiding it.

" Although the several dykes whicn have baen met with in all the working collieries of the present day, are accurately represented on the working plans of these collieries, yet, from the detached and local nature of those plans, no general and accurate notion of their lines of direction, bendings, and throws, can be formed from such detached sources of information. Nothing can effect the object of gaining an accurate knowledge of this important feature in the geological structure of our district, but the construction of a map of it, laid down from actual survey, on which all the dykes that have been yet discovered, shall be correctly represented. This map to be accompanied by a book of sections, showing the throws of the.

* Natural History Society of Northumberland, Durham, and Newcastle upon Tyne, at which society the paper from whence this extract is made, was read December 20th, 1830, and has since been published in Volume I. of the Transactions.

dykes in every part of the district. The promotion of such an undertaking is worthy of the most serious and prompt consideration of the society, as well as of the patronage of the landed and mining proprietors of the country."

It would be easy to multiply testimonies of this kind, but the general facts of the present imperfect state of mining plans and records, and the great utility of their being improved, are generally admitted. It is equally certain, that notwithstanding the frequent and earnest appeals of the very highest practical, as well as scientific, authorities, little has been done towards effecting any material amendment in this department of science. One of the objects of this work is to elucidate a particular mode of projection which has not hitherto been generally practised, and, indeed, is scarcely at all known in the districts of which I treat; and this precludes any lengthened details on mining plans &c. as commonly constructed. But assuming that the period is not far distant when an improved and scientific record of subterranean operations will be deemed indispensable, and as isometrical perspective is only one among many improvements, it may be desirable to offer some general observations on the subject; and in so doing I shall, for the sake of clearness, and for greater facility of reference, arrange these observations under separate heads, as follow :—

I. COLLECTION OF EXISTING DATA.

II. GEOLOGICAL SURVEYS.

III. GEOLOGICAL PLANS AND SECTIONS.

IV. PRESERVATION OF MINING PLANS AND RECORDS.

V. GEOLÓGICAL MAP OF THE NORTH OF ENGLAND ;

And, in the subsequent portion of the work, proceed to illustrate the application of isometrical perspective to this and other departments of planning, and to landscape and architectural drawing.

The first and most obvious step towards improvement in mining records is, to collect and arrange, with a view to their permanent preservation, all existing plans and details of subterranean works.    Many plans of collieries and lead mines are sufficiently intelligible to the viewers or surveyors who have constructed or are familiar with them; but different modes of representing similar objects, vague and indefinite descriptions, or a total absence of writing or lettering, and the want of connection with the true meridian or other permanent objects, with other similar imperfections, render such plans much less valuable and important as records, than they would be, if constructed with a rigid and undeviating regard to these particulars. It would be well if *uniformity of scale and conventional signs*, could be generally adopted for plans and sections in the respective districts of the coal and lead mines of the north of England. Such uniformity would be a most important point gained, towards obtaining that " knowledge of our subterranean wealth," which an eminent authority has justly observed, " would be the means of furnishing greater opulence to the country, than the acquisition of the mines of Mexico and Peru."

An arrangement of this kind would be found to possess material advantages, even as relates to the usual working plans of collieries and lead mines; but in some of the following sections of this essay, still further inducements to such uniformity will appear, and which are submitted as having some claims to the immediate attention of the conductors of mining establishments.

It affords me sincere pleasure to be able to state, that these and other practical suggestions which occur in the present work, relative to geological surveys and plans, have the full concurrence and approval of the experienced miner to whom this work is inscribed. In submitting them to Mr. Buddle's consideration, I found myself anticipated in some of the principal of them, by that gentleman's sound knowledge and long experience of practical mining, and from the prosecution of which his important and incessant avocations had alone deterred him. And since in all recommendations, which involve a departure from established usage, a shadow of doubt may reasonably attach, especially in the minds of those who are not fully conversant with details, it is necessary to add, that the subject in question has not only occupied a large share of attention as immediately connected with my profession, but that my opinions have ever been in abeyance to the full and impartial information which I have had many opportunities of gaining, both in the lead and coal districts of the north of England.

The large and unwieldy rolls of paper on which the workings of collieries and lead mines are often projected, might, I conceive, (except in a few particular instances,) be entirely dispensed with. Such plans (and the same applies to plans of estates) soon become so cracked and defaced, as greatly to impair the clearness and accuracy of the delineations, while their bulk militates against that frequent inspection and continuation of them, which would be readily effected on plans of less magnitude. So far as my own observation of subterranean plans and sections extends, I am of opinion that imperial drawing paper is sufficiently large for preserving a clear and methodical series of working, and other plans, and that, with a few occasional exceptions, all mining plans and sections might be delineated in squares of 20 inches, forming a superficial area of 2 ft. 9$\frac{1}{3}$ in., or, when unavoidably larger, in duplicates or quadruples of that area.

Fig. 1., plate I., represents the relative proportion of a square of 20 inches on a page of imperial drawing paper; an inch margin is left at the top and bottom, 3 inches at one end for binding a series of plans into a volume, leaving at the other end a margin of one inch, and a column 5 inches wide for the insertion of those written descriptions, scales, title, references, and other explanations, which will form a material feature of any improved system of plans, and with which the plan itself ought to be encumbered as little as possible.

The scales of geological and mining maps, so far as practical utility in any particular district is concerned, may be considered as varying from 2 miles to an inch to 1 chain to an inch.    On the former, which is suited to the representation of a large tract of country, the square of 20 inches would represent a district 40 miles square, including an area of 1600 square miles ; while on the latter scale, which is the largest in common use, the same space would include a portion of land a quarter of a mile square, or a superficial area of forty acres. The following are the intermediate scales most commonly adopted, with the area in miles, acres, roods, and perches, represented by one square inch, and by the entire square of 20 inches, according to the several scales :—

| NO. | Length represented by one inch. CHAINS. | | Area represented by one square inch. MILES. | A. | R. | P. | Lineal extent represented by the side of 20 in. MILES. | | Area represented by the square of 20 in. MILES. |
|---|---|---|---|---|---|---|---|---|---|
| 1 | 1 | - | .. | | | 16 | - | ¼ - | ·625 |
| 2 | 2 | - | .. | | 1 | 24 | - | ½ - | ·25 |
| 3 | 3 | - | .. | | 3 | 24 | - | ¾ - | ·5625 |
| 4 | 4 | - | .. | 1 | 2 | 16 | - | 1 - | 1· |
| 5 | 5 | - | .. | 2 | 2 | 0 | - | 1¼ - | 1·5625 |
| 6 | 6 | - | .. | 3 | 2 | 16 | - | 1½ - | 2·25 |
| 7 | ·8 | - | .. | 6 | 1 | 24 | - | 2 - | 4· |
| 8 | 10 | - | .. | 10 | 0 | 0 | - | 2½ - | 6·25 |
| | MILES. | | | | | | | | |
| 9 | ¼ | - | | 40 | 0 | 0 | - | 5 - | 25· |
| 10 | ½ | - | ¼ | 0 | 0 | 0 | - | 10 - | 100· |
| 11 | 1 | - | 1 | 0 | 0 | 0 | - | 20 - | 400· |
| 12 | 2 | - | 4 | 0 | 0 | 0 | - | 40 - | 1600· |

The comparative size of objects on plans, according to the respective scales, is frequently neglected. In some instances, and especially in very small scales, it is necessary to enlarge certain objects, as houses, roads, adits &c., in order to render them clearly discernible ; but when the scale exceeds 10 chains to an inch, the strictest regard should be paid to the comparative magnitude of objects. As a suitable accompaniment to this table, and for the better illustration of the value of each scale, representations are given in plate II. of the following objects projected on the above scales :—

1. An adit or level, 5 feet wide.
2. A shaft, 10 feet in diameter.
3. Coal workings, viz., *winning headway* 2 yards wide, *boards* 4 yards wide, *pillars* 8 yards square, and *thirlings* or *walls* 2 yards wide.
4. A road, 40 feet wide.
5. A lane, 20 feet wide.
6. A house, 40 feet long by 20 feet wide.
7. Plantation.

The squares on which these are drawn represent areas of one square acre, and the several objects are distinguished by the figures here annexed to each.

Before constructing any sections or plans, the scale ought to be very carefully considered, for on a proper selection of this, the clearness and beauty of plans greatly depend. As this selection,

B 3

especially in surveys of roads, estates, pleasure grounds &c., is often referred to gentlemen who are not practically conversant with such details, it may be useful to add a few remarks concerning the scales which are most suitable for such plans.

ONE CHAIN TO AN INCH.—This may be considered as the largest scale used in plans of land, roads, and mines, and is adopted only when they are very limited in extent, or when great clearness and accuracy is required. By the preceding table it may be seen, that by this scale a plan, 20 inches square, includes an area of 40 acres, and the quadruple of this, forming a plan of 3 feet 4 inches square, would consequently represent an area of 160 acres. For plans of valuable building ground, and for portions of roads, mines, &c., to be produced as evidence, &c., this scale is very proper, as it affords space for very clear illustration, both by ornamental drawing and writing. For plans of large gardens, pleasure grounds, and the several buildings thereon, the scale of 1 chain to an inch is very suitable. The square A B C D, Plate II, represents a square acre on this scale, with the several above-named objects drawn on it, in their respective proportions. The walls and apartments of a house may be represented on this scale, and the several plots and divisions of gardens and lawns, together with trees, hedges, &c., may be finished so as to have a good pictorial effect. Adjoining this square at A E F, is a delineation of coal workings on this scale.; but it is very rarely that any occasion exists for their being plotted so large.

TWO CHAINS TO AN INCH.—This is a very clear and expressive scale for land, where the extent is not such as to render a plan unwieldy. Where the area is less than five or six hundred acres, it may be adopted, especially if great accuracy and frequent reference for measuring distances, &c., is required; but for general use, half this scale combines sufficient clearness, and is four times as portable. The scale of 2 chains per inch is very commonly used for the working plans of collieries and lead mines, and is the least scale by which sections can be projected to be useful for practical purposes. The plan and section, Plate III, are projected on this scale, which renders the profile of the ground sufficiently clear without any increase of the vertical scale. For working sections of roads, railways, &c. this horizontal scale, with a vertical scale of 20 feet to an inch, is sufficiently large.

THREE CHAINS TO AN INCH is seldom used. When the scale of two chains is considered too large, it is desirable, if possible, to adopt that of

FOUR CHAINS TO AN INCH. This is much used for plans of estates, and exhibits the several fields,. roads, houses, &c., with sufficient accuracy for general purposes of reference. It is also fre-- quently adopted for mineral plans, and though, with care in the plotting of them, subterranean operations may be so clearly and distinctly defined by it as to give sufficient data for a permanent record, yet it is more suitable for a plan of a mineral district, than of the several workings of a particular mine.

This scale is the most valuable of any for com- bining clearness and minuteness of detail, with a considerable area, a plan of 20 inches square being equivalent to one square mile, and the moderate size of 3 ft. 4 in. square representing four square miles, or 2560 statute acres. It is also valuable for the ease with which it may be reduced or enlarged, *twice* this scale being the largest commonly used for working plans of mineral ground, and *half* of it corresponding with the scale of 10 inches to a mile, which is very suitable for large districts, and for working plans of roads ; while the half of this, or 5 in. to a mile, is a scale much used for parliamentary plans of extensive roads, railways, &c. This facility of enlargement or reduction is of great consequence, and will be still more so whenever any regular and methodical system of recording mining operations shall be generally adopted.

Of lesser scales than those here described, a comparative idea may be formed from the plate. With care, a scale so small as 16 or even 32 chains to an inch, may be employed for small plans of estates. In preserving plans of estates and farms in a book, it is desirable to adhere as much as possible to one scale; for the eye, deceived by the relative appearance of plans of different scales, is apt to form either very vague, or very incorrect ideas of their true proportions: 32 chains per inch will include an estate of 800 or 1000 acres on an octavo page, and a farm of 2 or 3 hundred acres may be very clearly delineated on a similar page, by a scale of 16 chains per inch. Specimens of plans drawn to these respective scales, are annexed, by way of illustration as to the clearness of delineation which they admit of, and which are more particularly explained in the descriptive references which accompany the plates.

The following are the scales which might be generally adopted for mineral plans, and which would admit of easy reference from one to another, in the enlargement or reduction which must often be required in preserving mining plans. The table in page 20 showing the areas included by the respective scales, affords a ready means of judging what scale is best adapted for any particular object, so as to be included in the dimensions suggested at page 19.

General Plan of a Mining District, showing not only the property, &c., immediately connected with any mine, but also a considerable extent of country around it : 8, 16, or 32 *chains to an inch*, according to the required area of land, and also to the adoption of the square of 20 inches, or the duplicate or quadruple of it, for the size of the plan.

Plan of Collieries and Lead Mines, with surface objects in detail, and general plans of the principal subterranean operations, 4 *chains to an inch*.

Working Plans and Sections of Coal and Lead Mines, 2 *chains to an inch*.

Occasional Sections in detail, showing minute workings or strata, &c., 1 *chain to an inch*.

Next to *uniform scales*, the adoption of *common conventional signs* is of the greatest consequence.   These may vary in different parts of the kingdom, owing to different strata, modes of working, &c. ; but it is well worthy of the attention of land and mine owners in the north of England, to effect *uniformity in their plans and sections*, the value of which, as an index to, and record of, their mineral property, would be exceedingly great. The owners and all other persons interested in such property, would thus be able to gain a clear understanding of the plans of them. Engineers or viewers from other parts, could readily form an exact idea of the nature and extent of the several workings; each new manager would at once become acquainted with what had formerly been done, while successive generations would profit by invaluable stores of information, and would thus transmit, from age to age, legible records of a subterranean world of wealth.

Plans of mines are, for practical purposes, carefully constructed from time to time in the offices of several collieries and lead mines. That the importance of preserving these should be not only admitted, but strongly urged, by the very best authorities, and that no regular system of doing so has hitherto obtained, are matters which it is difficult to reconcile. Plans after plans have been lost or destroyed, which, if now in existence, would be of infinite value, and which might have been preserved at an expense infinitely short of any thing like commensurate with the value of possessing such data concerning the mineral wealth of a district. An intelligent mining director has informed me, that plans and sections of

the old workings in a district under his management, would have saved many thousand pounds;
and such, from the causes already mentioned,
must ever be the result of neglecting this important department of practical mining.

An indifference to what is no less matter of
private and commercial interest than of public
duty, is probably destined not to continue in an
age when the minutest branches of science and
natural history are deemed worthy of arduous and
persevering pursuit, of costly publications, and
of promotion by public societies and subscriptions.
Botany and ornithology have, in particular, been
rendered delightful objects of general interest and
admiration; and geology, as a science, has also
made rapid advances in public favour. But those
minute practical details, from which alone any
important benefit or solid information can be
derived, are considered by many as devoid of
interest, and useful only in the private office
of mining agents. Geology and mineralogy,
form a wide field of investigation and enquiry, and
collections of accurate plans, sections, and drawings
form the surest guides to the study of them; they
are the alphabet by which the hidden and mysterious structure of the earth is unfolded to our
view, and if properly arranged and preserved,

will in time form a language not only intelligible
and interesting as a subject of general information,
but also as an important auxiliary to practical
mining.    The same Wisdom that formed the
smiling landscape, and the lofty mountain, formed
also the subterranean foundation on which they
rest.    Nor is the one less worthy of enquiry and
admiration than the others.  Those who admire the
gay plumage of the bird, or the attractive beauties
of the garden, will find in mineral treasures fresh
objects of beauty and variety, and the study of
which has an additional claim on attention by
its connection with local and national prosperity,
as well as with interests which are dear to every
breast, the interests of humanity.

## GEOLOGICAL SURVEYS.

In surveys of mineral districts, there are two
things which require particular attention.    The
first is a knowledge of the true meridian, the other
is a reduction of the undulations of surface, or
hypothenusal lines, to a horizontal base.    Great
difficulty and confusion are often created by inat-
tention to these most essential points in surveys
for purposes of practical mining.    Many old plans
are rendered almost entirely useless for want of a
true meridian on them, and the necessity of a

careful regard to the latter appears from the following illustration :—

Suppose a line to be measured for about two miles and a half in length, over a summit of 500 feet, and the angles of inclination (such as commonly occur, especially in mining districts) to be as follows :—

| Hypothenuse. Chains. | Angle of Inclination. | Base. Chains. | Difference. Chains. |
|---|---|---|---|
| 10 | 8° 7′ | 9·90 | ·10 |
| 20 | 4° 3′ | 19·95 | ·05 |
| 5 | 18° 12′ | 4·75 | ·25 |
| 5 | 0° 0′ | 5·00 | ·00 |
| 5 | 11° 29′ | 4·90 | ·10 |
| 16·50 | 14° 4′ | 16·005 | ·495 |
| 5 | 25° 50′ | 4·50 | ·50 |
| 25 | undulating | 24·97 | ·03 |
| 30 | 8° 7′ | 29·70 | ·30 |
| 121·50 . | | 119·675 | 1·825 |

The error arising from this example (which occurs on Whitley Fell, in Northumberland) is 120 feet 6 inches, or by a working scale of 2 chains to an inch, an error on the plan of nearly one inch, which, in subterranean works, might cause serious inconvenience, and, under some circumstances, occasion even fatal results.

In every mining district it is most desirable

that all difficulty in ascertaining the true meridian should be at once removed by the erection of two or more conspicuous objects placed exactly on a meridian line, which, after being projected with the most rigid accuracy, would remain as a permanent reference. Some prominent objects already existing might in some cases be selected; such, for instance, as the tall spire on Gateshead Fell, which is seen from a great portion of the colliery districts in the neighbourhood. This measure is indispensably necessary before any general system of preserving mineral plans can be adopted with that accuracy which can alone render them of value as a record from year to year, and from age to age. This is the very least that can be done to facilitate improvement in geological surveys, but it would be a work of infinite advantage to the prosperity of mining countries to have MERIDIAN LINES CAREFULLY SET OUT AT DISTANCES OF ONE MILE FROM EACH OTHER, AND TALL POSTS OR CURROCHS PLACED ON THESE MERIDIAN LINES AT EVERY MILE IN LENGTH, the undulating surface of the country being truly reduced to a horizontal base, so that these posts or stations should indicate squares of exactly one horizontal square mile. When rivers or other objects occur to prevent such posts being erected, the proper situation of them might be

indicated by three or four marks placed at equal
distances from them.  The most important part of
a district might be thus divided into square miles,
and any one of these lines could at any time be
continued in north, south, east, or west directions,
so as to make a connection with other parts of
the district.

This suggestion may appear novel, and perhaps
savour more of theory than practice to many;
but if acted upon, it would indisputably furnish a
most perfect and invaluable basis for mineral
surveys; and I am fully persuaded that the
advantages would immeasurably exceed any expense attending the adoption of such a plan.
The course of veins and dykes could then be
delineated through the several portions of a
district with a degree of accuracy which can
never be gained without such a basis.  Even for
surface plans these stations would be of great
utility; and when an exact survey of one of these
square miles was completed, all existing plans of
the mines, &c. beneath it could be delineated on
one or more copies of the plan, according as
different seams of coal, or different *randoms* of
vein workings might require, and all future surveys
could be plotted exactly in their relative position
to the former plans.

An infallible test of the accuracy of plans would

thus be obtained, and subterranean plans might be relied on with a degree of certainty which is now unthought of; which is unattainable without some means of easy and constant reference, such as is here suggested, and which must inevitably be more required as mines become deeper and more expensive to work.

The undulation of surface being truly reduced to a horizontal base in setting out these stations, it follows, that in all future surveys, the same must either be carefully attended to, or the error will soon appear. The method commonly recommended for making this reduction is to allow so many links to each chain, by pulling it forward before measuring the next chain length. This is attended with much inconvenience, especially where frequent off-sets or dimensions are required. The following mode is what I have found most useful for delineating plans of hilly ground, viz. : to mark the several angles of inclination in the field book, measuring the inclined the same as a plain surface, that is, without making any reduction of links from each chain, as commonly practised. Then, in plotting the line, these angles of inclination are first to be set off by a protractor, and the several lengths drawn according to their respective inclinations, with the position of the several fences, houses, or other objects. This

c

will form a profile of the country, from which the horizontal distances may be transferred by perpendicular lines let fall upon the original horizontal base line, which may be done with great ease and facility, by means of two German parallel rulers, the use of which will be more particularly explained in describing the projection of surveys by isometrical perspective.

This method saves a great deal of time in the survey, and preserves not only a profile or section of the surface, but also the relative position of the several walls, &c. on it; and all such sections ought to be carefully preserved, especially when isometrical plans are adopted.

### GEOLOGICAL PLANS AND SECTIONS.

Geological plans may be divided into three classes : the first comprising popular plans of a kingdom ; of a district, such as the north of England ; or of a county, or any considerable tract of country.   These must of necessity be delineated on a small scale, but, however small the scale may be, too much regard cannot be had to minute and exact delineations of the objects represented thereon.   Of such maps, and of the construction and publication thereof, I shall have occasion to speak more particularly in a following section, relative to a geological map of the north of England.

The second class are those plans of a mining district which have greater pretensions to accuracy than the first class, being on a clear and distinct scale, and constructed either from actual survey or accurate plans; these form a medium between the first class and the large working plans of mines. It is such intermediate plans that are best adapted for an arcana of geological and mining records, combining portability with tolerably accurate details. The third class consists of the large working plans and sections of mines.

The plan of a mining district should contain no objects but what are carefully laid down from actual admeasurement. These, on the surface, should be confined to the station currochs, and other prominent objects, especially on high lands. (See p. 31.) The position of shafts or other entrances to mines, the exact situation of every external indication of dykes, veins, and of the principal strata, and such rivers, fences, &c. as may be sufficient guides for ascertaining the relative position of the subterranean works; the lesser divisions of property, as fields, &c., being delineated on a plan of the surface only; the whole of the lines surveyed, however irregular the surface, should be projected on a true horizontal plane, without which all attempts to connect their position with the underground workings must be in vain.

A rigidly-accurate map of a whole district must necessarily be a work of considerable labour and expense, and would also require a long time for its execution in so minute a way as is here suggested ; but by means of the simple expedient of *station currochs on meridian lines*, any survey, however limited, would, by this connection with such stations, form materials which could, at any time, be laid down in the true relative positions, and after successive surveys had formed a skeleton plan of a district, the intervening spaces could be filled in at leisure, or deemed worthy of a survey to complete the district.

On such plans, not only a ground plan of each colliery or lead mine should be delineated, but also the several strata and workings should be annexed on sections.    It is very usual to add, on the plans and sections now commonly made, many suppositious lines of strata, course of dykes, veins, &c., which, with neat drawing and lettering, render them more intelligible than a purely scientific plan would be.    In plate VI the representation is strictly limited to actual admeasurements.    Supposed lines of strata, &c., are merely indicated by faint dotted lines, and small letters of reference are added, which, by occupying little space, render the plan more clear for the delineation of the workings.

The plans and sections of Silver Band, and part of Hudgill Cross Vein Mines, Plates III and VI, are submitted as examples of a mode of representing the workings of lead mines. The scale is 2 chains to an inch, and the following are some of the practical details for constructing such plans:—

Large brass circular protractors, and feather-edged ivory scales, should be used, for projecting the principal bearings and dimensions,—the paper should be the best hard drawing-paper, and should on no account be wet for the purpose of stretching, nor should any plan be stretched on canvas *after* it is drawn. If plans are required on canvas, the paper should be mounted, and very carefully dried before the plan is begun, in order that the contraction in drying may not alter the lines. Very good pencils may be had of respectable stationers for 7s. per dozen; the degree of hardness commonly marked H H suits well for planning, and bears a fine point. Short lines should be drawn with an ivory rule, or with German parallel rules, a dexterous application of which will be found greatly to facilitate the construction of plans. Rulers for long lines should be of hard and plain Spanish mahogany, with a fiducial edge, the perfect straightness of which should be carefully ascertained

c 3

before using them.*    The greatest care should
be taken to clean steel drawing pens every
time they are laid away, and common ink should
never be used in them.    Deep and permanent
*inks*, of different colours, would be a valuable
acquisition for mineral plans, but for which
the best substitute is a solution of the cake
colours, as required.    Inks, or deep liquid colours,
would have the advantage of a uniform tint; and
the same, of course, applies to liquid colours for
plans generally.  The most useful colours for plans
and sections are as follow :—

For surface boundaries, levels and subterranean workings, Madder or crimson Lake, Indigo,
Prussian blue, Cobalt, Purple, Chrome yellow,
Gamboge, Burnt Italian earth, Indian red, Burnt
umber, Cologne earth, Burnt sienna.

On sections, the subterranean works may be
coloured the same as the workings on the corresponding ground plan, thus increasing the

* This is best done by drawing a line along the edge of the
ruler very steadily with a finely-pointed pencil, then laying the
ruler on the other side of the line, with the extremities exactly upon it, and drawing a line in the same manner; if the
ruler is true, these lines of course exactly coincide, but if it
is round or hollow in the slightest degree, the defect is made
evident, the distance between the two lines being double the
amount of the convexity or concavity.

clearness of reference from one to the other; and strata may be distinguished as follows :—

Alluvial soil, Sepia.

Argillacious strata, Neutral tint.

Silicious strata, Roman ochre.

Calcarious strata, Prussian blue.

Basaltic rock, Purple.

A little prepared ox-gall used with the colours distributes them more evenly on the paper, and prevents the difficulty which often arises from the smoothness or greasiness of its surface, but it is almost impossible to use it too sparingly.

Neat and distinct lettering is very essential in all plans, and particularly so in subterranean plans and sections. In order to acquire skill and facility of execution in this department, I would recommend young men studying the profession to follow a method which I adopted for a few years with great advantage. This was the keeping of a brief diary of time employed at different surveys, plans, &c., in Roman letters, and by this daily practice, I was soon enabled to *print* (as it is often called) manuscript lettering of any kind with great ease and quickness. A practice of this kind will be found amply to repay any one who will diligently persevere in it.

As the lettering is of great consequence in such plans as are intended to be preserved, two

things may be observed, 1st, that the explana-
nation by letters should be full and explicit; and
2nd, that it should not be crowded on the plan
or section so as to obscure any of the workings.
Both these advantages may be effected by the use
of figures, referring to an explanation at one side
of the plan.

The most material use of mineral plans is, to
show the exact extent and situation of the several
workings, whether in coal seams or veins of lead.
No. 1, Plate VII, represents a mode of delineating coal workings; and No. 2, on the same
plate, represents the workings of lead mines by
means of pen and ink dots and strokes.   I have
suggested these, in preference to colours, as being
more readily made, less liable to fade, and admitting of greater variety in expressing different
degrees of productiveness.    Thus the *dots* at A
denote an excavation where *no ore* has been obtained; the *small strokes* at B, where *small quan-
tities of ore* have been procured, but insufficient
to pay the expense of working; the *crossed
small strokes* at C, where the vein has been
*tolerably profitable;* and the *thick intersecting
lines* at D, where it has been *exceedingly rich.*
The distinction between a tolerably-productive
and very rich vein should be fixed at a certain rate
per bing, according to the times, and which rate

should be inserted on the plan.    Small figures or
references might also denote the working price of
such parts of mines as are left with ore in; and
thus correct information might be preserved of
many details which are now buried in oblivion,
and remain as much the objects of blind adventure,
as if they had never been explored.

With such plans, books of reference should also
be preserved, containing general information concerning the history, progress, and productiveness
of each mine, quality of coals in different seams,
&c.; and in the lead districts might be inserted,
at stated periods, the number of men employed,
the length of level driven, in what stratum, and
at what cost; the quantity of ore raised, with the
situation and price of raising it, and the condition
of the roof, sole, and forehead of vein workings,
which latter might be expressed in small columns,
by shaded lines drawn with a pen, the same as on
the plans.

### PRESERVATION OF MINING PLANS AND RECORDS.

Having already observed that plans of such
a size as to bind into volumes may, by proper
arrangement, be made sufficiently clear and distinct for most purposes; it remains a matter for
consideration with the directors of coal mines

how far the suggestion is applicable to their respective works.    So far as my own knowledge extends, I can speak with more decision concerning plans of lead mines than of collieries.    The subject is referred, with deference, to the superior judgment and experience of the many able viewers and' other gentlemen engaged in coal mines; but in order more fully to explain the system which I conceive is, in a great measure, capable of adoption in plans of coal workings, I will illustrate it by the following example and accompanying remarks.

Suppose the underground workings of a colliery extend over an area included in two miles in length, and two in breadth.    A working plan of these, 2 chains to an inch, would be nearly 7 feet square, or on the less scale of 4 chains to an inch, the entire plan would be $3\frac{1}{3}$ feet square. Now, a general plan of this extent, reduced so as not to exceed 20 in. square, would be on a scale of 8 chains to an inch, by which the boundaries of manors and estates, with fields, roads, and the principal subterranean workings, could be clearly drawn.    Each side of this plan might be divided into four equal parts, which being connected by lines from side to side, would divide the whole into 16 squares, which might be represented in a series of plans 20 inches square, following the general one, and would then be on a scale of 2 chains to an inch.    The relative situation of the workings would be rendered clearly intelligible by the first or general plan, and the workings in detail might be neatly and accurately laid down on the larger ones, which, having numbers of reference to the general plan, any required part of the mine could readily be found. This method of keeping plans would be peculiarly adapted to geological surveys, by means of meridian lines projected on the surface.    Four of these working plans would complete one square mile, and might at any time be reduced and transferred to a geological map of the district.

Another advantage of such plans is the following:—It often happens that workings are to be represented which lie either under or above other workings already delineated on a plan.    Where such instances occur, the 20 inch plan could easily be copied on similar squares, and the several workings represented with great facilities of reference both to the general map and to the other working plans of the same portion of the mine.

I have already referred to the cracked, defaced, and soiled appearance of large plans ; the colours become faded, and the writing illegible, by the constant wear and tear to which they are exposed while plotting new workings upon them; and even the tension of the paper, by long use and frequent rolling, is no inconsiderable hindrance to the accuracy of them. Besides, if any one will attempt to draw a square of only 20 inches extent, and then submit the angles, diagonals, and other dimensions, to a strict mathematical scrutiny, it will be found a work of greater difficulty, and requiring a nicer exactness, than is commonly supposed; and hence it may be inferred, how very liable large plans are to imperfections arising out of the ordinary obstacles to correct delineation. Few persons can form any adequate conception how difficult a task it is to measure a straight line over a tract of country; and if ever mathematical stations be projected in mining districts, it will be found no easy task to project them with corresponding accuracy on paper.*

* The following extracts, relative to the practical difficulties of geometrical drawing, are from "Adam's Graphical Essays," a work which cannot be too highly recommended as a useful and most intelligent guide to many subjects connected with mathematical instruments and surveying.

. "The drawing of a straight line, which occurs in all geometrical operations, and which in theory is conceived as easy to be effected, is in practice attended with considerable difficulties."—"If the two points be very far distant, it is

Whether, for such projection, lines of longitude, or lines parallel to a meridian in the centre of a district, would be preferable, requires consideration ; but in either case it would be useful to adopt one of the following means of obtaining a correct basis for the delineation of plans :—

Engraved borders, exactly representing areas coinciding with those of surface stations, and

almost impossible to draw the line with accuracy and exactness ; a circular line may be described more easily and more exactly than a straight or any other lines, though even then many difficulties occur.

" Let no one consider these reflections as the effect of too scrupulous exactness, or as an unnecessary aim at precision ; for as the foundation of all our knowledge in geography, navigation, and astronomy, is built on observation, and all observations are made with instruments, it follows, that the truth of the observations, and the accuracy of the deductions therefrom, will principally depend on the exactness with which the instruments are made and divided ; and that these sciences will advance in proportion as those are less difficult in their use, and more perfect in the performance of their respective operations.

" If any wish to see the difficulties of rendering practice as perfect as theory, and the wonderful resources of the mind in order to attain this degree of perfection, let him consider the operations of General Roy, at Hounslow Heath ; operations that cannot be too much considered, nor too much praised, by every practitioner in the art of geometry."— *See Phil. Trans. Vol.* 80.

having scales of miles, chains, yards, and feet engraved on the side column, as in fig. I, plate I, in which column also might be engraved, a title, with blanks, thus—" No. —, PLAN of —— ——, belonging to —— ——, drawn (date) from (actual survey, or former plans) by —— ——, under the superintendence of —— ——." Then, after the scales, might be engraved explanations of signs and colours used, and faint lines for sundry explanations, sketches of detail, sections of strata, or any other information.   On turning over such a book, it would at once be seen where the responsibility of correctness lay, and in any investigation or enquiries recourse could at once be had to the proper plan, and to the parties who constructed it.

But as drawing lines and squares with mathematical precision is somewhat difficult, engraving them is still more so.   The most certain mode of obtaining a test for such engraved squares and scales would be, by projecting them with perfect truth on a large brass or steel plate, and then, by small perforations, marking the several corners and divisions of the scales.   One such plate, if carefully preserved, would serve a whole district for many years.   These and similar details, however, belong to a more advanced period of geological surveys, and are here noticed only as affording

some data for the consideration of those more
immediately interested in the subject.

With respect to preserving plans and sections
of lead mines, I shall best explain my ideas by
one or two practical instances.

In November, 1828, being consulted by the
Hon. F. C. Annesley and Partners, concerning a
plan of Silver Band lead mine, in Yorkshire, I
submitted the following proposal to them :—

" I propose to furnish a correct plan of the workings of Silver Band mines engraved on copper-
plate, and accompanied with a printed reference,
provided the company subscribe for as many
impressions as there are partners (18); and I
also propose to continue the same at such future
periods as the company shall think proper.   The
price of the original will be 10s. 6d. each, and of
the future plans 5s. each.   The agent to be
responsible for the delivery of the plans to the
partners, and for payment for the said plans, which
will be sent to him free of expense."

During the same month, I made a careful
subterranean survey of the mine, which was
situated on the bleak and barren forest of Lune,
in Upper Teesdale, 20 miles from my residence.
I projected the plan on a scale of 1 inch to a chain,
making a ground plan of the veins and levels, with
the washing floors, &c., and also a section of the
several strata and workings.   These I engraved on

copper-plate, and, after colouring the impressions, forwarded them to the agent. The intention was, at intervals of one or two years, to add the new workings on the copper-plate, to colour those *new parts* only, leaving all the former workings in outline uncoloured, and hence, if continued every two years, say for ten years, each partner would have six plans, as follows :—

No. 1. Plan showing all the workings
      of the mine up to Nov.,1828, £0 10  6
— 2. Plan of the whole mine, the
      coloured portion showing the
      several level and other work-
      ings made from Nov., 1828,
      to Nov., 1830,................  0  5  0
— 3. Do. do., from Nov., 1830, to
      Nov., 1832,..................  0  5  0
— 4. Do. do., from Nov., 1832, to
      Nov., 1834,..................  0  5  0
— 5. Do. do., from Nov., 1834, to
      Nov., 1836,..................  0  5  0
— 6. Do. do., from Nov., 1836, to
      Nov., 1838,..................  0  5  0

                                    ─────────
                                    £1 15  6
                                    ─────────

This collection would preserve a record of the entire operations of the mine for 10 years in the hands of each partner, for an annual expense of three shillings and sixpence; and for clearness, accuracy, and cheapness, such a mineral record has not, I dare safely venture to affirm, been carried into execution in this, or, perhaps, any other mining country.

In this instance, the partners were fewer in number than in many lead mines, and the mine difficult of access.    Every possible economy was used, and though nine guineas for the original survey, and four or five pounds for subsequent surveys, could scarcely pay in one single example, where travelling expenses, carriage of instruments, &c., were as expensive as if several contiguous mines were to be surveyed, yet it is quite sufficient to show, that the adoption of mineral plans, even on the most perfect scale, when once begun and persevered in, forms a very inconsiderable item of expense in mining.    The present instance of supplying every partner with a plan being less than $\frac{1}{8}$ *per cent.* on the annual expenditure.

For another example, take Holyfield mine, which I engraved in like manner on a plate 24 in. by 12 on similar terms, and say—

28 Partners.—For original plan,

at 10s. 6d. ......... £14 14   0

Do.        For surveys and plans

every 2 years at 5s.,

28 partners, £1 5s.    35   0   0

£49 14   0

Being to each partner an annual cost of three shillings and sixpence per annum for the entire series.

If the mines of a district were regularly surveyed in this manner, not only the partners of the mine, but the Lord of the Manor, would be interested in preserving them ; and such engraved sections would also be invaluable illustrations for geological lectures, and for the instruction of young miners. Geological societies, in different parts of the kingdom, would also, probably, pay a moderate sum for such series of plans,* all which would contribute to the exactness and economy of a system of preserving mining records, and accomplish in the most perfect and scientific manner, a record of subterranean works, at once a useful guide to the present, and an invaluable legacy to future generations.

The unqualified approval of this mode of preserving lead mining plans, by several eminent practical and scientific geologists and miners, has

* The district in which Silver Band mine is situated is highly interesting to the geologist from its abounding with the stratified range of Basaltic rock, which forms so prominent a feature in the scenery of Upper Teesdale, and immediately above which, on the summit of Cronkley scars, the operations of the mine were carrying forward at the time of this survey.

been gratifying to me; but domestic circumstances soon after called me from the district, and professional engagements have prevented me following up the endeavours which I proposed to make to effect an improved practice in this department of surveying in the lead mining district.   I am not without hopes that these endeavours may be of some future use, by calling attention to the subject; for though the above and similar instances barely repaid my actual expenses, they met with none of that opposition which *reform* of any kind, however desirable, is often destined to encounter.   On the contrary, from agents and many other gentlemen connected with mining, my enquiries and suggestions met with kind and friendly attentions which I shall ever gratefully remember, united as that remembrance is, with feelings of sincere regard and esteem.

About the same period (1828) I published some observations on the subject of preserving mining records ; the following extracts from which briefly explain the objects I had in view, and the mode of representation which I proposed to adopt in such plans.   The brief description of mines which accompanied them is also added, as explanatory of some of the examples given in this work.

" These plans exhibit the subterraneous workings of

the mines, by a HORIZONTAL or GROUND PLAN, and by
an UPRIGHT or VERTICAL SECTION ; the former exhibits
the course and bearing of the veins leased by each
company, and the levels, cross-cuts, drifts, &c., by
which access is had to the veins for procuring lead ore.
The section shows the order of superposition, and various thickness of the strata as they occur in different
mining fields, with the extent of the workings in them,
up to the date inscribed on each plan.   It is proposed
to add the subsequent operations at future periods
upon the same copper-plate, or, if necessary, on another plate, the impressions of which will be attached
to, and form a continuation of, the former.   The subsequent plans will have only those parts coloured,
which have been worked since the preceding date, and .
thus form a regular series of plans, exhibiting in a clear
and striking manner, a record of mining operations,
which can be furnished to every partner at the cost of
a few shillings for every 30th or 32nd share yearly, or
so often as from the extent of new workings may be
desirable.   As these future plans will not, in general,
exceed half the cost of the original one, it is suggested
that such a regular record of all the workings of mines,
placed in the hands of every partner at so trifling an
expense, would tend to increase their interest in, and
knowledge of mining affairs; facilitate their correspondence; and render clear and intelligible many subjects which, especially by distant partners, are often
imperfectly understood.

    " Those who are acquainted with the practical de-
tails of mining are well aware, not only of the utility

and convenience of having proper plans of the workings, but also of the great disadvantages and needless
expense often incurred by the want of them.   The engraved plans now offered to the mining proprietors of
Alston Moor, and to those interested in the study of
geology, continued in the manner above stated, would
obviate these difficulties, and, at the same time, furnish
to men of science a valuable fund of materials, derived
from authentic sources, and possessing both minuteness of detail and accuracy of delineation."*

"Geological plans and sections of mines have, from
a variety of causes, been much less generally attended
to, than their importance and utility demand.   Not
only do they afford very material assistance in the
actual prosecution of the works, but are further valuable from the minute and accurate geological information necessarily blended with them.   By supplying
numerous records of established facts, in the disposition and changes of strata, the position of veins, and
their productiveness under various circumstances, they
become admirable data for the study of a science, in
which a knowledge of facts, and a patient investigation
of practical results, are the only sources from which
any important discoveries can be derived."

"In the lead mining districts, the utility of such
records is increased by the non-residence of a large
portion of the shareholders of mines, who, without the
assistance of plans, and regular details, can only form
very imperfect ideas of the nature and objects of the

* Reference to Plans of Mines in the manor of Alston
Moor.

different works in progress.  These, in general, have had little or no opportunity of becoming conversant with such details, and are, therefore, naturally indifferent to the advantages which may be derived from them.  To many of these, it is anticipated, the plans now published will prove very acceptable, by affording both a general idea of the nature of mining, and of the manner in which its operations are rendered intelligible, by means of plans and sections.  And though such shareholders must necessarily place great reliance on the skill and integrity of their resident agents, and cannot, from occasional opportunities, acquire the knowledge of mining affairs requisite to the immediate direction of them; yet, in conducting such expensive speculations as mining, it is highly-desirable that the operations should be as far as possible made intelligible to all who take any interest in them.  Such a general knowledge as would enable them to understand the nature of the works, and the objects contemplated in any suggested undertaking, would be much more satisfactory than the entire dependence on others, induced by the want of means to form an opinion for themselves.

" The object of these plans is to furnish a clear and intelligible representation of the works earrying forward at the respective mines, and of the various strata in which they are situated.  By such plans of mines, accompanied with the correspondence of an agent or resident shareholder, the other proprietors, however distant, may at once perceive in what direction the works are proceeding, in what situations the veins are mostly found to be productive, and what are the most likely places for prosecuting new trials, both with reference to the intersection of veins, and the strata in which they may be conveniently tried.

"The following brief notices of some of the objects named on the sections are added for the use of those who are not familiar with the local terms used in mining, and which often occur in the correspondence of the agents of mines with non-resident proprietors.

"Veins are commonly named from the estate or tenement through which they pass, and neighbouring veins are often called north, middle, or *sun* veins, according to their situation—the latter term is commonly used by miners for south.

"Cross veins traverse the country in nearly a north and south direction, and are so called for distinction from other veins, the greater number of which have their bearing nearly east and west.

"The hade of veins is their leaning from the perpendicular, which varies much in different veins, and even in the same vein, being greatest in soft, and least in hard strata.

"The throw of veins is the disruption of the adjoining strata by which they have been raised or depressed on one cheek or side of the vein from the range of the corresponding strata on the other side; and it is a general, but not invariable feature, that veins hade or incline with their bottom to that side on which the strata are lower.

"Small veins are commonly called strings, and frequently accompany or diverge from larger veins.

"Flats are cavernous parts of the strata, occurring chiefly in limestone, in which ore and other mineral substances are sometimes found to extend in a horizonal direction on one or both sides of the vein, accompanied by numerous leads or small fissures, strings, &c. passing obliquely, or, to use a very common mining term, *swinning* through the vein.

" Levels are horizontal passages by which access is gained to the workings of the mine—those which form the principal entrance, and communication in the interior, have wood or iron rail-ways, and are called horse levels; when made for drainage they are called water levels. When levels occur on a plan having different *randoms*, that is, are on different horizontal planes, they are distinguished by different colours.

" Drifts are similar horizontal passages, either in the vein, or driven for discovery of veins, and ventilating the mine, &c. Cross-cuts are short drifts from the principal level to the vein. The extreme end of any level, drift, cross-cut, or working in the vein, or so far as it has proceeded, is called the forehead.

" A shaft is a pit dug from the surface—a rise is an upright working commenced from a level, drift, or cross-cut, and *worked upward*—a sump is exactly the reverse, being a shaft or pit *worked downward*, and commenced, not from the surface, but from some part of the interior of the mine. Rises and sumps are usually named after some of the miners who worked them.

" The boundary of veins leased in this manor varies in length, and in breadth commonly extends forty yards on each side of the vein.

" Lead ore, either pure or intermixed with other mineral substances, as it comes from the mine, is called Bouse, and is deposited in places called Bouse Teams; the refuse excavations form what are called dead heaps. The Bouse is afterwards broken into small pieces, either on knocking stones, by manual labour, or in the crushing mill by a water wheel; it then undergoes various processes in water at the washing floors, and the refuse of these operations is laid into *cutting heaps*. The sediment that escapes with the stream is collected in slime pits, and the ore contained in this sediment is afterwards separated from it by washing. The whole of the ore obtained, after being properly prepared by these various processes, is laid in depôts, called bingsteads, from whence it is removed to the smelting-house.\*

GEOLOGICAL MAP OF THE NORTH OF ENGLAND.

The several county maps which already exist of the northern counties of England, though answering most of the purposes of general reference, do not possess that degree of accuracy which is desirable for the ground work of a geological map of so important a district. This is not mentioned with any idea of disparagement to these publications, for it is quite beyond the

\* Geological sections of lead mines in Alston Moor and Teesdale, by T. Sopwith, land and mine surveyor, published October, 1829, and inscribed to John Taylor, Esq., F. R. S. F. G. S., &c.

means of any single individual, or of any limited company of persons to effect that extreme accuracy. To show, however, that this discrepancy is fatal to any dependance being placed on these and similar maps for minute purposes, such as the range of dykes or veins from one mine or district to another, &c. the following instances may be noticed, as occurring in a part of the county where such continuation of bearings, and the relative situation of different mines, &c. is of extreme importance, so much so, indeed, that in one instance, an error of even one yard in length would have involved a difference of nearly one thousand pounds.*

The mining manor of Allendale consists of two valleys, formed by the east and west Allen rivers. In two recently published maps of the county, *the distance of these rivers is a mile different* for nearly the whole extent of these respective dales.

From the mining village of Coalcleugh to that of Allenheads, on one map is $5\frac{1}{4}$ miles ; on the other, $3\frac{1}{2}$ miles, being a difference of $1\frac{3}{4}$ mile in this short distance.

* This was the well-known Rampgill vein, the workings of which were surveyed by the celebrated Smeaton, and the value of which, at its intersection with the boundary between Alston Moor and Allendale, was estimated at £1,000 per yard, in length.

The important boundary referred to in the note
from the north-east to the south-west extremity
of Alston Moor, on one map is 7½ miles, on the
other 5½ miles.

From the same north-east angle of Alston
Moor to a prominent angle of the county
boundary south of Allenheads, is on one map
11¼ miles, while the same points on the other
map are within 8¾ miles—these several distances
being all measured in direct lines from point to
point.

It is obvious that any conclusions drawn from
a geological map, projected on so erroneous a
ground work, must be of little practical utility.

A CORRECT GEOLOGICAL MAP of the three
northern counties would, indisputably, be a most
invaluable acquisition to science, mining, and
agriculture, while on such a map the insertion of
any material error would be open to local, and
probably minute investigation.

The following remarks on the subject are
offered with a view of drawing attention to that
accuracy, on which the value of any local geological
map must mainly depend.

A long period must elapse before the many
valleys, mines, &c. which abound in the mountainous districts of the three northern counties,
could receive any personal examination.    The

Basaltic range of rocks from Teesdale to Belford, the western escarpment of the Penine range of hills, the various rocks of the Cumbrian mountains, the Tyne and Wear coal-fields, and many other portions of these counties, would require much careful investigation before any authentic and minute plan of their geological structure could be made.

Without any further comment on the obstacles to speedily constructing geological county maps, I shall submit a few suggestions as to the most desirable mode of proceeding to illustrate the geology of these counties, and also concerning the ultimate completion of a large and correct geological map of the north of England.

By way of more clearly explaining my views, I venture to define a mode of proceeding, which, being merely offered for consideration, is, of course, open to every alteration and amendment that the opinions of others, or more mature experience, may suggest.

Supposing, then, the work fairly commenced either by the Natural History Society, or some public body, under the auspices of the great coal and lead owners; it follows, that access could be had to many plans of land and mines, with permission to reduce them to any required scale. The engraved plans of Greenwich Hospital estates, Rennie's plans of the Tyne and Wear, the large manor plans of Alston, Allendale, and Whitfield, and many valuable plans of extensive property in the Newcastle coal district, would be valuable materials for such a collection; while, I need scarcely add, how much the professional aid of Mr. Buddle, Mr. Wood, and other active and willing promoters of geological science, might add to these preliminary data.

When once the collection was begun, and the object of it fully understood, materials would rapidly accumulate. I would propose that the more important parts of the district should then be selected and completed into maps of convenient size, say 10 inches square, which, on a scale of $2\frac{1}{2}$ inches to a mile, would include an area of 16 square miles. Separate portions of which, on a larger scale, might also be drawn on plans of similar size, according to the geological details to be expressed on them.

Accurate plans of such portions of districts being obtained, I would recommend that they should be very carefully engraved.

Separate impressions of these maps should be coloured from existing geological maps—other impressions sent to gentlemen and mining agents residing in, or acquainted with such district, on which remarks and information might be inserted ;

while, from time to time, members of the society, conversant with geology and mining, might make scientific excursions, with copies of the maps in their hands, and thus record their several observations.

A few well-executed maps of this kind, constructed from these various sources of information, all brought as it were into one focus, would be of more real service than any general map of a large district can possibly be without such preliminary means of acquiring correct details.

Having in this manner accomplished maps of certain districts, the corrected details might be laid on the copper-plate plans, and the impressions being properly coloured might either appear in the transactions of the Natural History Society, or be published separately. Two such plans, with a plate of sections, and a few pages of descriptive letter-press, would be a neat and useful mode of arranging them into a series of geological plans.

A collection of fifty or sixty plans, comprising from 800 to 1000 square miles of the principal portions of the mining districts, with accompanying sections, drawings, and descriptions, would afford an admirable view of the geology of the north of England. Every portion of this series would present the results of careful personal observation, corrected by frequent enquiries and inspection.

Fresh discoveries could, at any time, be added on the plates, and how many opportunities might not the lapse of eight or ten years afford of gaining such accessions of knowledge. Repeated visits of scientific men, the opening of quarries, the sinking of shafts, borings, &c., might in this period tend to clear many difficulties which must be encountered, and perhaps very imperfectly overcome, in any attempt to construct at once a detailed geological map of so 'vast an extent of country.

The publication of a series of maps would, I imagine, tend far more to promote an acquaintance with, and general interest in geology, than that of a single large map. The letter-press, sections, and drawings, of each number, would be interesting to the public of each respective district. Many would examine, and learn to understand a map of the geological structure of the place in which they live, who would deem a county geological map far beyond either their interests or comprehension; and a printed cover of these numbers might also be a useful vehicle for publishing the nature and advantages of the ultimate objects in view.

When, at length, a great number and variety of materials, manuscript or engraved, shall have been collected; when one portion of the district after another has been submitted to careful revision ; when the published plans have benefited by criticism and amendment ; when geological plans and sections have, at a moderate expense, been rendered familiar to the public eye ; when charts of coasts, maps of parishes, plans and sections of mines, roads, and railways, and various data, shall have accumulated in the portfolios of the conductors of the undertaking ; when these and similar advantages shall be accomplished, the construction of a large geological map may then be proceeded in with a degree of precision and utility which cannot otherwise be attainable.

To the advantages already enumerated may be added the very important one, that previous to such general map being constructed, the ordnance surveys of the north of England may probably be completed. If to this were added the projection of meridian stations over the mining districts, the work would be complete.

A map thus constructed, would possess accuracy of delineation, and minuteness of detail, commensurate with the importance of the districts comprised in it ; would assuredly reflect the highest credit on the conductors of it ; and form such a specimen of geological planning as has not hitherto been accomplished.

## CHAPTER II.

# ISOMETRICAL PROJECTION.

PERSPECTIVE is the art of delineating on a plane
the appearance of objects according to the laws
of vision. Every one who is at all conversant
with drawing, knows that perspective lines con-
verge so that near objects may seem large, and
distant objects small; and that, in like manner,
according to what is called aerial perspective,
the colours of near objects are strong and clear,
while those of distant objects are faint and
indistinct. The proper diminution of the size
and colour of objects, according to their distance,
and to the relative position of the eye, is, therefore, what is commonly understood by perspective;
the principles and practice of which have been
explained in numerous works, and a knowledge
of these principles and modes of application is
not only of great interest as a scientific pursuit,
but in many circumstances is quite indispensable
as a matter of business. True perspective is the

E

nearest approach that can be made to the figures which objects assume in that inimitable picture which is formed on the retina of the eye, and of which the images produced by the Camera Obscura afford the clearest illustration ; but it is obvious that for many practical purposes, the diminution of ordinary perspective renders such drawings extremely intricate, and incapable of. admeasurement.  To avoid this obvious difficulty, recourse has been had to artificial modes of representation, which, though less accordant with the actual appearance of objects, yet possess the properties of representing the *real* and not the *apparent* shape of objects, and of being conveniently measured in several, if not in all, directions.

It would be far from the object of the present work to enter into any abstruse speculations on the several modes of projection employed in constructing maps and geometrical drawings ; a subject, to the proper consideration of which the limits of this volume would be inadequate.  The public are in possession of many excellent publications on perspective.  Nothing, however, has been published in the form of a treatise as even relates to *parallel projection*, which is so necessary in the delineation of plans, elevations, sections, &c, And here I may observe, that probably no person in this kingdom has rendered more essential service to practical geometry, nor more successfully elucidated the principles of mathematical projection, than my respected friend, Peter Nicholson, Esq., for whose liberal and intelligent communications on such subjects I cannot but express my highest acknowledgments.

To enter on the full consideration of the subject of projection, would not only occupy a considerable space, but would also involve a departure from the design of this publication, which is to offer a practical view of the subject as connected with mineral plans and surveys, and with the delineation of land and buildings in landscape, architectural, and mechanical drawings.*   And

* A treatise on projection is a desideratum in English literature, and certainly no one is more eminently qualified to supply the want than Mr. Nicholson, whose works on practical carpentry and other subjects, form an invaluable arcana of practical geometry, and contain, in detached passages, the most scientific explanations of the theory and practice of projection which have hitherto appeared.   Orthographical projection, as regards the circles of the sphere, has been long known, but its application to solids in general was imperfectly understood, until Mr. Nicholson introduced a general method in Rees' Cyclopædia, in the year 1813, where the application is shown in various difficult examples of the projection of solids, particularly the dodecahedron.   This method possesses the advantages of being extremely simple in its principles, and universal in its application ; nor in the writings of either continental or English authors has any

since every mode of projection which is convenient
for frequent and extensive application, must of
necessity be extremely simple in practice, as well
as theory, it is desirable to confine any explanation
of the subject to such plain and obvious particulars, as may be readily comprehended by every one
in the numerous class who are interested in such
drawings ; and in the following pages some of
the leading demonstrations and most useful
problems connected with the subject will be introduced, as further illustrations for those who prefer
a geometrical consideration of the principles and
practice of Isometrical projection.

Highly-important and ingenious as many modes
of projection undoubtedly are, little experience
in the delineation of objects is required to show
that PARALLEL PROJECTION is not only the most
useful method of representing objects, but is
almost the only one which has ever been generally
adopted for plans of land or mines, or for architectural and working designs for buildings and
machinery.   With this mode of projection every
one is familiar, by the names of the GROUND PLAN
AND SECTION, as applied to land or strata, and of
PLANS and ELEVATIONS as applied to buildings.

other general method been proposed.  An example of its
application to the projection of a cube is shown in Plate
XII.

These ground plans, sections, and elevations, are, in fact, true representations of the relative size and position of objects which are exactly situated on *one plane* surface, as (in a geometrical sense) they would appear if viewed from an infinite distance. When, therefore, fields or any objects are situated on *one uniform plane*, this orthographic mode of representation furnishes what may be called a *perfect miniature resemblance*, *every dimension* and *every direction* being in exact proportion to, and coincidence with, the subject represented. No sooner, however, does any deviation from the plane occur, than this beautiful similitude of the orthographic representation ceases. Thus, for instance, the undulating surface of a hilly country, or the inclination of roofs, &c., cannot be truly shown on a ground plan, but are more or less distorted according to the angles which they make with the plane on which the drawing is projected. This inconvenience results from the nature of vision, and cannot by any mode of representation be entirely avoided. In few words, it may be observed, that the great advantage and simplicity of the ground plans, sections, and elevations in common use, consist in this :— That ONE SCALE is applicable *to every part* and to *every direction* of the plane represented, an advantage exceedingly great, and

E 3

which no other species of projection possesses.
The principal disadvantage is, that the connection of one plane with another cannot be
shown but by separate drawings, which for many
purposes are less explanatory than those modes
of projection which exhibit two or more planes
combined in one drawing.

This may be readily understood, from the example of a cube, the sides of which may be
exactly represented by separate squares, which,
however, cannot be united in their relative position
in one drawing, and hence an oblique or perspective view affords a clearer idea of the construction of this solid, and of the relative position
of its sides.    Plate IX. represents three sides
of a cube, each of which is 165 feet square.
Fig. 1 is an orthographic projection or ground
plan of the surface;  Fig. 2 represents a vertical
section of the strata lying directly under the line
A B ;  Fig. 1, and the section under the line B C
is represented in Fig. 3.    Now each of these
forms the most perfect representation of each
respective side that can possibly be drawn;  and
if joined at right angles, the side a b to the line
A B, and the side b c to the line B C, a model
would be produced of the top and two sides of a
cube, which, if the drawing were correct, would
form a miniature fac-simile of the objects repre-

sented, and would convey a faithful idea of the relative position of these several objects better than any other means that can be used. Now, as it is in many cases extremely desirable that the relative position of different planes should be shown, the most obvious method which suggests itself is, to form a representation of such a model, as it appears from a point which commands a view of the three different sides, and to do this, the aid either of *perspective* or *projection* is required.

By PERSPECTIVE a cube may be represented so that one, two, or three sides may be seen in any variety of position, according to the supposed situation of the eye of the observer. If, then, it is required to show all the three sides equally, the place of the eye must be in the direction of the diagonal of the cube produced, for this diagonal is the only line which forms an equal angle with any three adjoining faces of a cube. But if the eye is supposed to be at any finite distance, the further sides of each square will be diminished by the laws of perspective, as at Fig. 3, Plate XII, which shows the appearance of a cube of 3 feet (of which Fig. 6 is one side) when viewed in the line of the diagonal produced, at a distance of 12 feet from the nearest angle. Fig. 4 represents the same cube at 24 feet distance, and Fig. 5 as it would appear at 48 feet distance. From these examples it is very obvious that such perspective drawings could never be extensively used for plans and sections, since, except the edges, every other part of them would require a different scale. The apparent form of Fig. 5 is evidently better adapted for planning than the distorted lines of Fig. 3, the greater distance of the former making the angles of diminution to be so small as to cause little deviation from the true *geometrical figure* of the same cube, as it would appear if viewed from an infinite distance (see Fig. 7). The mode of representation which this supposition of an infinite distance effects, is called PROJECTION, and by it a cube or any other figure may be delineated in *any position* without *any perspective diminution* of the several parts according to their distance, since all the parts are necessarily considered as being equally distant. But though the varieties of projection are as innumerable as are the possible combinations of the distance and positions of the objects represented, yet a combined view of horizontal and vertical planes in one drawing, and all capable of being measured by one scale, can only be delineated by one mode of projection, viz. : as viewed from an infinite distance in the direction of the diagonal of a cube produced, or, in other words, in a direction forming an angle of 35° 16′ with the plane of the horizon. *Any*

*other position,* as viewed from *any distance,* may
indeed be represented with geometrical truth,
and may also be measured by different scales
suited to the several planes ; but the least acquaintance with practical delineation will show
that, however well adapted some of these projections may be for some particular purposes,
they are altogether unsuitable for the extensive
and general application required in geological and
mining plans, to which isometrical projection is
the only one that can be rendered generally applicable.

This projection, for which, as relates to plans
and sections, so exclusive an excellence is claim-
ed, results from such obvious principles of geometry, that no recognition of it in modern times
can reasonably claim as a discovery what must
have been co-existent with the earliest knowledge
of geometry. The origin of isometrical projection
is at least co-existent with the inscription of a
hexagon in a circle, for if all the opposite angles
of a hexagon be joined by straight lines, a perfect
isometrical representation of a cube is thereby
produced; but while these few obvious geometrical *principles* claim so great antiquity, their
application to projection is altogether modern.
In an able paper in the first volume of the Cam-

bridge Philosophical Transactions, the general nature and usefulness óf isometrical projection are elucidated by Professor Farish, who, without entering into detailed geometrical disquisitions, gives a clear and intelligible view of the subject, and also suggests the appropriate name of isometrical perspective.    This paper has had a greater and well-deserved publicity given to it in Dr. Gregory's " Mechanics for Practical Men."    It was through the medium of this latter work that my attention was first directed to the subject, and being at that time engaged in mineral surveys of a highly-interesting district, I constructed an isometrical drawing, exhibiting some of the most curious mining and geological sections of the district.    This I believe to be the first application of isometrical projection in the mining districts of the north of England, and several highly-intelligent mining engineers have concurred in thinking the method well adapted for many purposes of geological delineation.    To buildings it has been more generally applied, and examples of it may be seen in Louden's publications on agriculture, &c. ; yet the value of this mode of drawing is not generally appreciated, and hence, at the suggestion of Mr. Buddle, the present work has been undertaken, with a view to its practical exposition, and more especially as relates to geological and mining plans and sections.

Isometrical projection exhibits three *conter-minous* or adjoining sides of a cube, having its under side on the plane of the horizon ; see Fig. 7, Plate XII. Each of the three sides appears of equal size and shape, and *all the edges*, or boundary lines, are of equal length. In each side, two opposite angles are 120° each, and the other two opposite angles of each side are 60° each. The three angles formed at the corner nearest the eye, which is in the centre of the figure, are each 120°. All the opposite boundary lines are parallel, and all lines drawn parallel to any of these boundary lines, will coincide with them, and may be measured by *one common scale*. By isometrical projection, *all perpendicular lines* may be measured by *the same common scale*, and *by no other mode of projection can all the edges of three sides of a cube be represented on paper, or any flat surface, so as to be measured by one scale.* This brief enumeration of some of the properties of isometrical projection, will be readily comprehended by referring to the figure of a cube so represented. A clear idea of these properties will enable any one to understand the practical application of them as explained in the succeeding chapters of this work ; and having endeavoured to convey to the general reader some knowledge of the nature of perspective, projection, and of iso-metrical projection, the following illustrations of the latter, contributed by Peter Nicholson, Esq., will be still more explanatory to a numerous class of readers :—

### ELUCIDATION OF THE PRINCIPLES OF PROJECTION.

The shadow of an object by the sun upon a plane perpendicular to its rays is the orthographical pro-jection of the contour of the object, and if in solids comprised under plane surfaces, we construct, or suppose to be constructed, a frame or cage of wires, which shall form the same angles, and which shall have the same proportion to one another as the edges of the solid, the shadow of the frame by the sun upon a plane perpendicular to the rays of light would be the ortho-graphical representation of the linear edges of the solid, and exactly what ought to be drawn when the position of the object to the plane of projection is known. And if the wire frame were similarly constructed to the edges of a solid comprised under rectangular planes, and the sun's rays parallel to the diagonal of a cube, which has its edges parallel to those of the wires, the shadow of this frame would be the isometrical projection of the linear edges of the solid.

Moreover, if in a point at a limited distance from the object, the flame of a candle be supposed to be con-denced, the shadow of the wire frame by this light, upon a plane behind it, would be the perspective representation of the linear edges of the solid; and if the light were in the diagonal produced of a cube similarly situated to the wire frame, and the plane of the picture perpendicular to this diagonal, we should have the isometrical perspective representation of the linear edges of the solid.

Isometrical projection combines the uses of perspective and geometrical drawings of plans, elevations, and sections. It is of equal utility with perspective in showing how the parts of a design are connected together, and has this advantage over it in exhibiting the measures of those parts.

Much study is required, in order to carry a complex design which is represented by geometrical drawings into execution, from its being necessary to represent the object by as many separate drawings as it has faces. Hence the advantage which isometrical projection has over geometrical drawings, in uniting all the faces of an object; and, consequently, representing the object itself by one drawing.

Isometrical projection will either enable the artist to execute a design according to the intention of the designer, or the draughtsman to make such a drawing of an object or objects already existing, whether land, machinery, or buildings, as will exhibit to another the measures and positions of the things represented.

Though isometrical projection is most readily applied to those objects which have all their faces rectangular, it may easily be adapted to others situated in, or referable to any of the rectangular planes of the faces of the solid.

The word projection is used by writers in a general sense, either for the perspective or for the orthographical representation of an object. The celebrated Brook Taylor, in his new principles of linear perspective, uses the word *projection*, and the words *perspective representation*, as synonymous, viz. the former in the sense of the latter. Other writers on perspective, who have not treated of orthographical projection, have used the same expressions indifferently for the perspective figure of the object. To avoid this ambiguity, the word projection* is here used to signify orthographical projection, and perspective representation for the figure of the object or objects in perspective.

It is absolutely impossible to find the projection of a solid when the figures of the faces, and the angles which the planes of these faces make with one another, are given by any other method than the one alluded to in the note, page 67, except the figures of the faces be all rectangles; and, even in this the most easy of all examples is far from having the simplicity of the new method, by finding the projection of each face separately, by means of the intersecting line of that face with the plane of projection.

Many have confounded the principles of orthogra-

* This is in conformity with the celebrated French writers on descriptive geometry, which is a method that enables the artist to determine, by means of two planes of projection, one perpendicular to the other, the positions and lengths of the lineal parts of solids orthographically represented upon each plane in the manner of a plan and elevation, which, when one of the planes of projection is parallel to the horizon, this plane is called the horizontal plane of projection, and the other is called the vertical plane of projection.

phical projection with descriptive geometry; but the principles are entirely different, inasmuch as the former requires only one plane of projection, and the latter* requires two.

Professor Farish was the first to observe, that in projecting solids comprised under rectangular faces, that if the projecting rays were parallel to the diagonal of a cube having its faces parallel to the faces of the solid to be projected, he would be enabled, by a common scale, to draw the representation without the trouble of actual projection, in such a manner that all the right angles would be represented in the drawing either by angles of 60° or 120°, and that all the right lines or edges of the solid would be represented by right lines which would have the same proportion to one another as the corresponding edges of the original.

It was from this circumstance that Professor Farish denominated the projection arising from the diagonal position of the projecting rays ISOMETRICAL PERSPECTIVE; the substantive perspective, however, is not so strictly applicable as projection, for perspective implies

---

* Descriptive geometry applies to the solution of problems in space, in a similar manner as plane geometry to the solution of problems described upon a plane surface; thus, for instance, plane geometry shows how to let fall a perpendicular from a given point to a given right line; and descriptive geometry shows how to let fall a perpendicular from a given point in space to a plane, and to find the point in which the line meets the plane, the two projections of the plane, and the two projections of the point from which the perpendicular must pass, being given. This cannot be done without the use of two planes of projections, one perpendicular to the other, as stated in the preceding note.

a representation of an object by rays proceeding from the solid to *a point at a limited distance,* and in their progress intercepting the plane of the picture; whereas in projection the rays are supposed to be parallel, and consequently would never meet in a point as in perspective. It is therefore proper to substitute *projection* for *perspective,* and to call this mode of projection isometrical projection.

Isometrical projection, though not adapted to the delineation of such bodies as the regular solids, the general projection of the sphere, the intersections of cones, cylinders, spherical surfaces, &c., is of the greatest importance in delineating by far the most numerous, useful, and convenient forms of solids, namely, those comprised under rectangular faces.

The principles of ISOMETRICAL PROJECTION may be thus arranged :—

That species of orthographical projection in which the projecting rays are parallel to the diagonal of a cube, and the edges of the body to be projected parallel to the edges of the cube, is called ISOMETRICAL PROJECTION.

The three edges of the cube which meet each other in the diagonal, are called CONTERMINOUS EDGES.

The three faces of the cube which meet each other in the diagonal, are called the CONTERMINOUS FACES.

The diagonal of a square which meets the diagonal of the cube, is called the CONTERMINOUS DIAGONAL.

One of the triangles, which is made by dividing the diagonal parallelogram into two parts by a diagonal which is the diagonal of the cube, is called the DIAGONAL TRIANGLE.

The orthographical projection of any portion of one of the edges of the solid to be delineated, is called the ISOMETRICAL LENGTH of that portion.

The things to be drawn are called BODIES, SOLIDS, OBJECTS OR ORIGINALS, and the pictures are called REPRESENTATIONS, FIGURES, IMAGES or PROJECTIONS.

## PROPOSITION I.

The sides of any one of the diagonal triangles of a cube are in the ratio of $\sqrt{3}$, $\sqrt{2}$, $\sqrt{1}$.

### Fig. 1., Plate X.

For, let ABCDEF be a cube.   Draw the diagonals AH and GD of the squares BAFH, CGED, and join AD; then AD is the diagonal of the cube.

Because AG and HD are perdendicular to the planes BAFH, CGED, the figure AGDH is a rectangle which is divided into two equal right-angled triangles AGD, AHD, by the diagonal AD of the cube.

The two sides which contain the right angle of each of these triangles, consist of the side and diagonal of a square; hence if the side of the cube be 1, the side of each square will be 1; and (by Eu. B. i. p. 47) the diagonal will be $\sqrt{2}$; therefore, the legs of the diagonal triangle will be 1 and $\sqrt{2}$; hence (by Eu. B. 1. p. 47) the hypothenuse or diagonal of the cube will be $\sqrt{3}$; therefore, the hypothenuse, the base, and perpendicular of this diagonal triangle are in the ratio of $\sqrt{3}$, $\sqrt{2}$, $\sqrt{1}$, that is, in the ratio of 1, $\frac{1}{3}\sqrt{6}$, $\frac{1}{3}\sqrt{3}$, or as 1, ·81649, ·57401.

## PROP. II.

The angle made by the diagonal of a cube and any

F

one of the three conterminous edges, is equal to the greater of the two acute angles of the diagonal triangle.

*Fig. 2., Plate X.*

For, draw the diagonal AD of the cube, dividing the rectangle ACDF into the two diagonal triangles ACD, AFD, equal to one another. Now DAF is the angle made by the diagonal AD of the cube and the edge AF; but in the diagonal triangle AFD, the side DF is greater than AF; hence the angle DAF is greater than ADF. Therefore the proposition is manifest.

Coroll. Hence the angles made by the diagonal of the cube, and each of the three conterminous edges, are equal to one another.

## PROP. III.

The angle made by the diagonal of a cube with any one of the three conterminous diagonals, is equal to the less of the two acute angles of the diagonal triangle.

*Fig. 2, Plate X.*

Now DAC is the angle made by the diagonal AD of the cube and the conterminous diagonal AC; but in the diagonal triangle ACD, the side CD is less than AC; hence the angle CAD is less than CDA ; hence the proposition is manifest.

Coroll. 1. Hence the angles made by the diagonal of the cube, and each of the three conterminous diagonals of the squares, are equal to one another.

Coroll. 2. Hence the diagonal of the cube is equally inclined to each of the three conterminous faces of the cube.

## PROP. IV.

The diagonal of a cube is perpendicular to a plane drawn through three points in the conterminous edges, at equal distances from the vertix.

*Fig. 3, Plate X.*

For, join BF, FG, GB, and let the diagonal AD intersect the plane BFG in *a*, and through *a* draw GJ, FK, BL, to meet BF, BG, FG, in the points J, K, L, and join AJ, AK, AL.

Now the sides· *a*A, AB of the triangle *a*AB, are respectively equal to the two sides *a* A, AF of the triangle *a*AF, and the angle *a*AB of the triangle *a*AB has been shown (by p. 2) to be equal to the angle *a*AF of the triangle *a*AF; therefore (by Eu. B. i. p. 4) the sides *a* B, *a* F, are equal to one another; similarly the sides *a* G, *a* B, are equal to one another; therefore, *a* B, *a* F, *a* G, are equal to one another; and because BF, FG, GB, are equal to one another, the triangles B *a* F, F *a* G, G *a* B, are (by Eu. B. i. p. 8) equal to one another, and the angles contained under the equal sides are equal to one another; therefore the angles B *a* F, F *a* G, G *a* B, are equal to one another; and the remaining angles are equal to one another; and because the two sides KF, FB, and the angle KFB of the triangle KFB are respectively equal to the two sides KF, FG, and the angle KFG of the triangle KFG, the base KB is (by Eu. B. i. p. 4) equal to the base KG, and the angle FKB equal to the angle FKG; therefore, (by Eu. B. i. de. 10) the angles FKB and FKG are right angles; therefore BG is bisected in K, and similarly FG, BF, are bisected respectively in L and J.    Moreover, because the three sides AB, AK,. KB, of the triangle AKB are respectively equal to the three sides AG, AK, KG, of the triangle AKG, the angles AKB, AKG, are (by Eu. B. i. p. 8) equal to one another; therefore, each of the angles AKB, AKG, is (by Eu. B. i. def. 10) a right angle, and since the angles *a*KB, *a*KG are right angles, the right line BG is (by Eu. B. xi. p. 4) perpendicular to the plane AKF; therefore, (by Eu. B. xi. p. 18) the plane AKF is perpendicular to the plane BFG, and similarly the planes of the triangles ALB, AJG are perpendicular to the plane BFG; therefore, the common section A*a* is perpendicular to the plane BFG; hence the proposition is manifest.

## PROP. V.

Any one of the three conterminous semidiagonals is to its projection in the ratio of $\sqrt{3}$ to $\sqrt{1}$, and any one of the three conterminous edges is to its projection in the ratio of $\sqrt{3}$ to $\sqrt{1}$.

### *Fig.* 4., *Plate X.*

For AK is half the conterminous diagonal of the square ABCG, and AF one of the conterminous edges.   Since AD or A*a* is perpendicular to the plane BFG, the triangles A*a*K and A*a*F are right angled at *a*, and since the angle DAF is equal (by Prop. ii.) to the greater, and the angle DAK equal (by Prop. iii.) to the less of the two acute angles of the diagonal triangle, the triangles A*a*K, A*a*F are similar to the diagonal triangle;

Therefore, in the triangle A$a$K, AK : $a$ K : : $\sqrt{3}$ : $\sqrt{1}$
and in the triangle A$a$F, AF : $a$ F : : $\sqrt{3}$ : $\sqrt{2}$

But since the plane KAF* is perpendicular to the plane of projection BFG, and since A$a$ is (by Prop. iv.) perpendicular to the plane BFG, $a$F is the projection of AF, and $a$K the projection of AK. Hence the proposition is manifest.

## PROP. VI.

The isometricals of any two lines are in the same ratio as the lines themselves.

*Fig. 5., Plate* X.

For on the edge AB take any distance AC, and on the edge AG take any distance AD, and draw C$c$ and D$d$ parallel to A$a$, meeting $a$B in $c$, and $a$G in $d$.

Since A$a$ is perpendicular to the plane BFG; therefore BFG may be the plane of projection; but the planes A$a$B, A$a$F, A$a$G, are each perpendicular to the plane BFG, therefore $a$B, $a$F, $a$G, are respectively the projection of the conterminous edges AB, AF, AG. Moreover, $ac$ is the isometrical of AC and $a$ $d$ of A D.

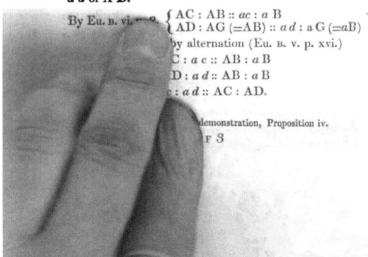

By Eu. B. vi. $\left\{\begin{array}{l} \text{AC} : \text{AB} :: ac : a\,\text{B} \\ \text{AD} : \text{AG}\,(=\text{AB}) :: a\,d : a\,\text{G}\,(=a\text{B}) \end{array}\right.$

by alternation (Eu. B. v. p. xvi.)

C : $a\,c$ :: AB : $a$ B
D : $a\,d$ :: AB : $a$ B
$c$ : $a\,d$ :: AC : AD.

demonstration, Proposition iv.

r 3

## PROP. VII.

The angles formed by the isometricals of three conterminous edges of a cube are equal to one another, and the sum of the three angles equal to four right angles.

*Fig. 6., Plate X.*

For $a$B, $a$F, $a$G are (by P. vi.) the isometricals of the three conterminous edges AB, AF, AG, and the angles B$a$F, F$a$G, G$a$B, are equal to one another, and at the same time equal to four right angles; hence the proposition is manifest.

## PROP. VIII.

In an ellipse, which is the projection of a circle in one of the faces of the cube, the semi-axis major, the isometrical radius, and the semi-axis minor are to one another in the ratio of $\sqrt{3}$, $\sqrt{2}$, $\sqrt{1}$.

*Fig. 7., Plate X.*

Let RSTU be a circle in the plane of the face ABG or ABCG, and let A be the centre, and let the circumference of the circle intersect AB in R, and AK in S. Draw the radius AT parallel to BG, and draw R$r$, S$s$, T$t$ parallel to A$a$; then will $r$ be the projection of R, $s$ the projection of S, and $t$ the projection of T.

Since AT is parallel to BG, the projection $a\,t$ of AT is parallel to BG, and equal to AT the radius of the circle; and since AK and $a$K are perpendicular to BG, $a\,s$ is perpendicular to $a\,t$; hence $a\,t$ is the semi-axis major, and $a\,s$ the semi-axis minor, and $a\,r$ the isometrical radius of the circle.

By the triangle A$a$B, ............... AR : $a\,r$ :: $\sqrt{3}$ : $\sqrt{2}$

And by the triangle A $a$ K, A S(=AR) : $a\,s$ :: $\sqrt{3}$ : $\sqrt{1}$

Let A R=$\sqrt{3}$; then will $a\,r = \sqrt{2}$, and $a\,s = \sqrt{1}$; hence A R, $a\,r$, $a\,s$, are in the ratio of $\sqrt{3}$, $\sqrt{2}$, $\sqrt{1}$.

## PROP. IX.
To draw the diagonal triangle.
*Fig* 1., *Plate XI.*

Draw the two right lines YX and YZ perpendicular to each other. From the point Y with any convenient distance, YZ taken on one of them, cut the other in the point $v$, and from the same point Y, with the distance Z$v$, cut YX in X. Join XZ and XYZ is the triangle required.

For if YZ, the side of a square, be 1, then Z$v$, the diagonal of the square, which will therefore be equal to $\sqrt{2}$, that is XY is equal to $\sqrt{2}$; and, therefore, since in the right angled triangle XYZ the side YZ is 1, and the side YX is equal to $\sqrt{2}$, XYZ is the diagonal triangle.

## PROP. X.
To find the isometrical projection of a circle, the isometrical projection of the centre, and that of the radius of the circle being given.
*Fig. 2., Plate XI.*

Let RS be the isometrical scale of feet. Let the diameter of the circle be 6 feet, and let $a$ be the projection of the centre.

Through the centre $a$ draw the isometrical lines *hg*, *fi*, *bc*, and draw *de* perpendicular to *bc*. Take 3

feet from the scale RS, and apply it upon the side YX
from Y to p of the diagonal triangle XYZ, Fig. 1. Draw pq
parallel to XZ meeting YZ in q.   From the centre a,
with the distance pq, cut de in the points d and e,
again from a with the distance Yq cut bc in the points
b and c.   With the two axes de and bc describe the
ellipse bdce, which will be the isometrical projection of
the circle required.

## PROP. XI.

To find the isometrical projection and the perspective representation of a cube, the linear edge being
given.

### Fig. 1., Plate XII.

Assume any convenient point a for the projection of the centre of the cube, draw the right lines
aK, aL, aM, making angles of 120° with each
other, make any one of them aK of any convenient
length, and make any other of them aL equal to aK.
Prolong Ma to A, from the point P where MA intersects KL, make PA equal to PK or PL, and join AK.

From the point A, with a length equal to the linear
edge of the cube, cut AK in B, and draw Bb parallel
to Aa, meeting aK in b.   From the point a, with the
distance ab, cut aL in d, and aM in f.   Complete the
parallelograms abcd, adef, afgb, and the figure abcdefg
is the projection required.

Draw aq parallel to KL, make aq equal to the linear
edge of the cube, and from the point K with the distance KA cut KL in p.   Draw pq cutting aK in b',
from the point a with the distance ab', cut aL in d', and
aM in f'.   Draw d'K, f'K to the vanishing point K,

*b'*L, *f*'L to the vanishing point L. *b'*M, *d'*M to the vanishing point M, and the figure *abc'd'e'f'g'* formed by the intersections of the lines drawn to the points K, L, M, will be the isometrical perspective representation of the cube.

The side of the cube thus perspectively represented, is one half of the distance of the eye, so that if the distance of the eye were 6 feet, each side of the cube would be 3 feet.

In order to render the process of projection evident, make *a*M equal to *a*K or *a*L, and join LM and KM, then the triangle KLM will be equilateral. Prolong K*a* to A', and L*a* to A". Let KA' intersect LM in Q, and LA' intersect KM in R. Because the angles of the equilateral triangle KLM, are bisected by the right lines M*a*, K*a*, L*a*, those three lines produced will bisect the opposite sides KL, LM, KM in the points P, Q, R, at right angles; hence PK, PL, QL, QM, RK, RM, are equal to one another, and PA was made equal to one of these equal lines; make QA' and RA" each equal to the same length. Join AL, A'L, A'M, A"K, A"M, and the triangles KAL, LA'M, KA"M will be right-angled at the points A, A', A", and the sides AK, AL, A'L, A'M, A"K, A"M will be equal to one another. From A' with the distance AB cut the line AL in D', and from A" with the same distance cut the line A"K in B". Upon AB describe the square ABCD, upon A'D' describe the square A'D'E'F, and upon A"B" describe the square A"B"G"F".

Suppose this construction to be made upon thick drawing paper, and let the rectilineal figure KALA′ MA″K be cut out from the paper. By the edge of a ruler, and with a pointed instrument not quite sharp, draw the lines KL, LM, KM deeply impressed, but not cut through, so that the surfaces on each side may turn with ease. Revolve the triangles KAL, LA′M, KA″M upon KL, LM, KM until the points A, A′, A″ coincide in one point A, and the figures KALA′M A″K will become a pyramid AKLM, of which the vertix is A, the base, the equilateral triangle KLM, and the sides isosceles triangles right angled at the vertix A, and, consequently, perpendicular to one another. The three squares ABCD, A′D′E′F′, A″B″G″F″ will form the three faces of a cube, of which the vertix is A, and the figures *abcd, adef, abgf* will be the projections of these squares; and, consequently, the entire figure *abcdefg* the projection of the cube.

In regard to the perspective representation, the plane of the picture is the plane of the equilateral triangle KLM, the point of sight is the vertix A of the pyramid, the centre of the picture is the point *a* in which the isometricals of the three conterminous edges meet each other. The three planes or faces which terminate in A, the vertix of the pyramid, are not three conterminous faces of the cube, as in the case of the isometrical projection, but are in planes parallel to these faces of the cube; hence the sides KL, LM, KM, of the equilateral triangle KLM are the vanishing lines of the three conterminous faces, and K, L, M, are the vanishing points of the three conterminous edges; the real cube being supposed to be behind the picture, and to have its vertix in the centre. Hence the representation may be found by the common principles of perspective.

In order to conceive how isometrical projection may be applied to represent objects situate upon the plane of the horizon, we have only to imagine any one of the three faces of the pyramid which contains one of the faces of the cube to coincide with the plane of the horizon, then the faces of the cube adjacent to its base will become vertical; and, consequently, the upper surface parallel to the horizon, and the plane of projection, which contains the equilateral triangle KLM, will make an angle with the plane of the horizon equal to 54° 44′ as we have before stated.

Fig. 2, Plate XII, is a scale one quarter of an inch to a foot.

Figures 3, 4, 5, exhibit the representation in perspective of a cube 3 feet in each of its linear dimensions. In Fig. 3, the distance of the eye is 12 feet; in Fig. 4, 24 feet; in Fig. 5, 48 feet. Fig. 6 exhibits the square of one of the faces of the cube; and Fig. 7 is the isometrical projection of this cube. All these figures are proportioned by the scale Fig. 2. Fig. 8 exhibits the same representations as in Figures 3, 4, 5, and 7, with the addition of another perspective representation viewed at the distance of 6 feet, all contained within one another. The continued approach, as the distance from the eye to the picture is increased, of the perspective representations towards the isometrical projection is obvious. But to render this still more so to the understanding, the length of the linear side of the cube in perspective

Viewed at 6 feet distance is 1·900* feet.

| | | | |
|---|---|---|---|
| at | 12 | ... | 2·140 | ... |
| at | 24 | ••• | 2·284 | ... |
| at | 48 | ... | 2·364 | ... |
| at | 96 | ... | 2·406 | ... |
| at | 192 | ... | 2·427 | ... |

The length of the isometrical edge of the cube will be found to be 2·449 feet, (see note); the differences between this length and the successive perspective lengths will, therefore, be ·549, ·309, ·155, ·085, ·043. ·022 decimal parts of a foot. Since this series of differences is continually approaching to a geometrical

---

* When the distance of the picture is 1, the distance between the eye and each vanishing point is $\sqrt{3}=1·73205$, and the distance between the centre of the picture and each vanishing point is $\sqrt{2}=1·41421$. Therefore these numbers, being multiplied by the distance of the eye in feet, yards, &c., will give the distances from the eye, and from the centre of the picture to each vanishing point in feet. Thus,

*Distance of the vanishing Point.*

$\begin{cases} 6 \times 1·73205 = & 10·39230 \text{ feet from the eye.} \\ 6 \times 1·41421 = & 8·48526 \text{ feet from the centre of the picture.} \end{cases}$

$\begin{cases} 12 \times 1·73205 = & 20·78460 \text{ feet from the eye.} \\ 12 \times 1·41421 = & 16·97052 \text{ feet from the centre of the picture.} \end{cases}$

$\begin{cases} 24 \times 1·73205 = & 41·96920 \text{ feet from the eye.} \\ 24 \times 1·41421 = & 33·94104 \text{ feet from the centre of the picture.} \end{cases}$

$\begin{cases} 48 \times 1·73205 = & 83·13840 \text{ feet from the eye.} \\ 48 \times 1·41421 = & 67·88208 \text{ feet from the centre of the picture.} \end{cases}$

$\begin{cases} 96 \times 1·73205 = & 166·27680 \text{ feet from the eye.} \\ 96 \times 1·41421 = & 135·76416 \text{ feet from the centre of the picture.} \end{cases}$

$\begin{cases} 192 \times 1·73205 = & 332·55360 \text{ feet from the eye.} \\ 192 \times 1·41420 = & 271·52832 \text{ feet from the centre of the picture.} \end{cases}$

progression, in which the last term will be half of the preceding one, we may easily anticipate the difference between the isometrical length of the edge of the cube and the perspective length at double the last distance of the eye, by the simple operation of taking the half of the last difference. Hence the difference between the isometrical edge of a cube, 3 feet in each dimension, and the perspective length of the edge, when the distance of the eye is 384 (=2×192) feet, is ·011 (=·022÷2) decimal parts of a foot; and if the distance of the eye were 768 (=2×384) feet, the difference would only be ·005 (=·011÷2). Hence the difference between the isometrical edge of a cube, 3 feet in dimensions, and the perspective edge, when the distance of the eye from the picture is 768 feet, is only $\frac{5}{1000}$ part of a foot, or $\frac{6}{100}$ part of an inch. Here we have only extended the

Then to find the length of each of the edges add 3 feet, the side of the cube, to the distance between the eye and each vanishing point; then, by the principles of perspective, as the distance thus increased is to the distance between the centre and the vanishing point, so is 3 feet, the linear side of the cube, to its perspective length. Hence,

13·39230 : 8·48526 :: 3 : the perspective length.
23·78460 : 16·97052 :: 3 : —————————
44·56920 : 33·94104 :: 3 : —————————
86·13840 : 67·88208 :: 3 : —————————
169·27680 : 135·76416 :: 3 : —————————
335·55360 : 271·52832 :: 3 : —————————

These computations being made, we obtain 1·900, 2·140, 2·284 2·364, 2·406, 2·427 feet, the perspective lengths of the edges.

To find the isometrical length of each edge of the cube,

$$\sqrt{3} : \sqrt{2} :: 3 : \text{the isometrical length.}$$

Or, 1·73205 : 1·41421 :: 3 : the isometrical length of edge. This being found, will be 2·449 nearly.

decimals to third place of figures, presuming this number, in a practical illustration, will be sufficient.

The perspective representation of the cube will always be greater, as the distance of the eye is greater; but can never be increased so as to become equal to the isometrical projection; but if the isometrical projection were diminished in the smallest degree whatever, the perspective representation could thus be made to exceed it in magnitude.

### PRINCIPLES OF PRACTICE.

To make isometrical drawings of extensive grounds, containing buildings or other works of art, plantations, &c., we must imagine a horizontal plane, at a convenient distance, under the surface of the earth (as described in the sequel by Mr. Sopwith), and this plane to be reticulated with squares of a convenient size, we shall suppose, for the sake of easy reference, that the right lines forming these squares are parallel and perpendicular to a meridian line, and the cube to be placed upon the horizontal plane, with the sides of its base parallel to the sides of the reticulated squares. Then the diagonals of the cube will make angles with the plane of the horizon equal to 35° 16′ nearly, and will either point to the north-east, north-west, south-east, or south-west: we shall suppose that the plane of projection is perpendicular to the one pointing to the south-east, or to the other pointing to the south-west, then the plane of projection will decline 45° to the east or to the west, according as the diagonal of the cube points to south-east or south-west.   All upright or vertical lines in space will be represented by lines perpendicular to the base of the drawing; but the isometrical horizontal lines will vary their places on the right or left according to the declination of the plane of projection.

By means of the assumed horizontal plane, the artist will be enabled to exhibit objects and excavations both above and below this plane, and to show their real heights and depths according to any standard measure from the surface of the earth itself, as also their position on the horizontal plane.

The angle formed by the isometricals of any three conterminous edges being equal to one another, and their sum equal to four right angles, each of these angles will be 120°. Hence, if one of the isometricals be assumed, and a circle be described from any convenient point in this line cutting the line, and with the extent of the radius, from the point thus cut, the circumference be again cut on each side of it, right lines drawn from the centre through each of these points, and the isometrical before assumed, will divide the circumference of the circle into three equal parts. Since all the edges of a solid contained under rectangular planes are all parallel to the three edges of any solid angle, and since the projections of parallel lines are also parallels, having drawn the three first isometricals, every line in the representation will be parallel to one or other of these three lines, and may therefore be drawn by a parallel ruler.

The isometricals of any two edges of the solid being in the ratio of the edges themselves, the lengths of the isometricals may be proportioned by a scale of any convenient length, so that all lines in the drawing will have the same proportion to one another as the edges of the object. Hence if we suppose the scale to be equal to that of the object to be represented, every isometrical will be of the same length as that of its corresponding edge.

For though in reality, with regard to the object and its projection, the isometricals are less than the corresponding original edges in the ratio of $\sqrt{2}$ to $\sqrt{3}$, and though in making the design of an object isometrically, it is generally found convenient to represent it by a scale much smaller than that by which it is intended to execute the object; yet this relation has nothing to do with the design, as the work may be executed from the drawing according to the intention of the designer.

### ELUCIDATION OF THE PRACTICE OF ISOMETRICAL DELINEATION,
#### WITH A DESCRIPTION OF
### AN ISOMETRICAL PROTRACTOR, AND ITS APPLICATION.
#### DEFINITIONS OF LINES AND ANGLES.

1. An ISOMETRICAL LINE coincides with, or is parallel to, the edges of a cube viewed from an infinite distance in the direction of the diagonal of the cube produced.

2. An IN-ISOMETRICAL LINE is the projection of a right line not parallel to an isometrical line, situated in one of the three conterminous faces of the solid*, or in any plane parallel to these faces.

---

* See definitions, page 80.

3. An OUT-ISOMETRICAL LINE is the projection of a right line in space not parallel to any of the three conterminous planes.

4. An ISOMETRICAL ANGLE is one of which the containing sides are both isometrical lines.

Hence no angle can be an isometrical angle, unless it is the projection of a right angle.

5. An IN-ISOMETRICAL ANGLE is the projection of an angle in any of the three conterminous faces of the solid, or in any plane parallel to these faces.

6. An OUT-ISOMETRICAL ANGLE is the projection of an angle in a plane perpendicular to one of the three conterminous faces, but not parallel to any one of them.

7. A RIGHT-HAND ISOMETRICAL is an isometrical line in the drawing running obliquely upwards towards the right hand.

8. A LEFT-HAND ISOMETRICAL is an isometrical line in the drawing running upwards towards the left hand.

CONSTRUCTION OF THE ISOMETRICAL PROTRACTOR.

Fig. 3, Plate XI., is the isometrical protractor, of which the construction is as follows:—Upon any convenient indefinite right line, Fig. 2, Plate XV, and from any point in the line with the length of the tangent of 45°, cut the line on both sides of the point. (The tangent line used for this purpose ought to be taken from a well-divided scale.) Upon the whole extent of the line describe an equilateral triangle on each side of it, and the rhombus, including the areas of the two triangles, is an isometrical square, of which the common base is the shorter diagonal. Draw the remaining longer diagonal, which will intersect the other at right angles.

If the axis minor of the ellipse be determined upon the shorter diagonal, by placing the semi-axis upon each side of the centre, the longer axis may be found as follows:—From the centre O with the length of the semi-axis minor, cut the longer diagonal, and from the same point O with the distance between the point of section and the extremity of the shorter axis, cut the longer diagonal in a second point, then the distance between the second point of section and the extremity of the shorter axis is the semi-axis major. Hence from the centre O with the semi-axis major cut the longer diagonal on each side of the centre, and the distance between the points of section is the greater axis. Upon the two axis describe the ellipse, which will be the isometrical projection of a circle. The two diameters, AB and CD, which are parallel to the sides of the isometrical square, are called the ISOMETRICAL DIAMETERS of the circle. Then describe the two inner curves which comprise the divisions for the degrees.

Through the centre O draw two right lines parallel to the sides of the rhombus; these right lines will bisect the sides of, and each part will be equal to half the shorter diagonal.

From the bisecting point, on each side of it, with the consecutive tangents from 1 to 45 taken from the before-mentioned scale, cut each side of the rhombus successively. Place a straight edge upon the centre

O, and each point of division in each of the four sides of the rhombus, and mark the short lines of division between the two outer curves, and between the single degrees and the lines between the two inner curves, and between every ten degrees. When the divisions are all graduated, write upon every consecutive 10th degree from A to C, from B to C, from A to D, and from B to D, the numbers 10°, 20°, 30°,......90°, also from D to A, from D to B, from C to A, and from C to B, write 10°, 20°, 30°......90°, which, when done, will complete the construction.

Fig. 4, Plate XI, is another isometrical protractor, in which the line AB is applied upon both right and left isometrical lines.

The diameters AB and CD of the ellipsis forming the boundary of the protractor, are called its ISOMETRICAL DIAMETERS. All other diameters are called in-isometrical diameters; an ISOMETRICAL RADIUS is the half of an isometrical diameter, and an in-isometrical radius is the half of an in-isometrical diameter.

In making surveys by means of a circumferenter or magnetic compass, the position of every horizontal line whatever, is ascertained by means of a meridian line; hence the angles which horizontal lines make with one another may be found from the angles which each of these lines makes with a meridian. Therefore, in isometrical drawings it will be eligible to chose one of the isometrical lines for an isometrical meridian, and to prevent those mistakes which would arise by taking a right or left hand isometrical line at pleasure, we shall adopt the right hand line to be used as a meridian, which will be found sufficient to delineate isometrically all angles whatever situate in a horizontal plane, without having regard to the left hand line. However, with respect to the delineation of angles which represent angles in a vertical plane, right and left hand isometricals must be used occasionally, accordingly as the planes containing these angles are on the right or left hand.

## PROP. XII.

To draw an isometrical line from a given point, making an angle with an isometrical meridian, which shall be the projection of a right line on a horizontal plane perpendicular to the real meridian.

Place the isometrical diameter AB of the protractor under which is written RIGHT-HAND LINE HORIZONTAL PLANE, upon the meridian with the centre O upon the given point, and mark a point on the paper close to the curved edge at 90. Then having removed the protractor, draw a right line from the given point to the point at 90, and this right line will represent the perpendicular required.

## PROP. XIII.

To draw an isometrical line from a given point, making an angle with an isometrical meridian, which shall be the projection of a right line perpendicular to a horizontal plane.

Place the Isometrical diameter CD of the protractor, under which is written RIGHT-HAND LINE VERTICAL PLANE, upon the meridian, with the centre O upon the

given point, and make a point on the paper close to
the curved edge at 90. Then having removed the
protractor, draw a right line from the given point to
the point at 90, and this right line will represent the
perpendicular required.

## PROP. XIV.

At a given point in and with a given isometrical
meridian to delineate an angle, which shall represent
an angle in a horizontal plane containing any given
number of degrees.

Place the isometrical diameter AB of the protractor
upon the isometrical meridian, with the centre O upon
the given point, observing that if, in taking the angle,
the original line be on the west side of the meridian,
the line to be drawn must be placed above the isometrical meridian; but if the original line be on the east
of the meridian line, the line to be drawn must be
placed below the isometrical meridian; and if the acute
angle made by the original line and the meridian be
on the north, the degrees on the isometrical protractor
must be numbered from the end B of the isometrical
diameter pointing to the north; but if the acute angle
made by the original line and the meridian be south,
the degrees of the isometrical protractor must be numbered from the end A of the isometrical diameter pointing to the south. The position of the isometrical
angle being thus fixed, draw a curve line along that
part of the graduated edge which contains the degrees
of the acute angle required to be delineated. Having
removed the instrument, draw a right line from the

G 3

given point to the extremity of the curve in which the
number of degrees required terminate, and this line
will make the required angle with the isometrical meridian.

## PROP. XV.

At a given point in, and with a given isometrical
meridian, to delineate an angle which shall represent
an angle in a vertical plane containing any given number of degrees.

Place the isometrical diameter CD of the productor
upon the isometrical meridian with the centre O upon
the given point, observing, that if, in taking the original
angle, (which is always acute) the original line which
makes the angle with the meridian, be on the north, the
degrees to be taken by the isometrical protractor must
be those numbered from the end D of the isometrical
diameter pointing to the north; but, on the contrary,
the degrees must be numbered from the end C pointing
to the south. The position of the line forming the required angle with the isometrical meridian being thus
fixed, draw a curve line along that part of the graduated
edge which contains the number of degrees of the angle
required. Then having removed the instrument, draw
a right line from the given point to the extremity of
the curve in which the number of degrees required
terminate, and this line will make the required angle
with the isometrical meridian.

## PROP. XVI.

An in-isometrical angle, and the curve which is the

projection of an arc comprised by the two sides of the angle, being given, to find upon the in-isometrical side from the vertex a projected distance of 10, 20, 30, &c. feet, yards, chains, &c.

From the vertex with the distance required (of 10, 20, 30, &c. feet, yards, chains, &c.) taken from the isometrical scale, cut the isometrical side of the angle through the point of section, draw a right line parallel to a right line or chord joining the extremities of the curve to cut the in-isometrical side, and the distance intercepted upon this side between the vertex and the point of section is the projected distance required.

By this means any length may not only be projected, but a scale may be made, which scale will give any number of feet, chains, &c., upon the in-isometrical line.

*To find the scale by the proportional compasses.*

Set the distance between the points at one end, and the distance between the points at the other ends, so that these two distances may be in the ratio of the isometrical radius to the in-isometrical radius, observing, that if the isometrical radius be greater than the in-isometrical radius, the longer ends of the compasses must be adapted to the isometrical scale, but if less, the shorter ends must be adapted to the isometrical scale.

If the scale on the line of lines in the sector can be conveniently used as an isometrical scale, the scale for the non-isometrical line may be found in the following manner. Upon the line of lines set the isometrical radius from the centre of the joint, observing the division upon each bar upon which the extreme point of distance falls, contract or enlarge the angle of the sector until the distance between the observed points is equal to the in-isometrical radius, and the parallel distances between the like numbers 1-1, 2-2, 3-3, &c. will represent 1, 2, 3, &c., or 10, 20, 30, &c. of the scale adapted to the non-isometrical line.

## EXAMPLES.

Ex. 1. Delineate a crooked line of road-way, of which its different bearings and lengths in its consecutive rectineal parts are N15°W, 280 chains,—N60°E, 600 chains, and N25°E, 550 chains respectively.

Let A, Fig. 1, Plate XIII, represent the point of commencement of the operation. Draw AN for an isometrical meridian, the point N representing the north of the point A. Now observing that in this example AN and all its parallels are right hand isometrical lines; therefore, in protracting the angles of the various bearings, the edge AB of the isometrical protractor, under which is written RIGHT HAND LINE HORIZONTAL PLANE, must be the isometrical diameter of the ter of the protractor which is to be applied upon these parallels; and since the bearings are all north declining to the east or west, the degrees must be numbered from the north end B along the curved edge above or below the isometrical meridian accordingly as the declination is west or east.

Place the centre O of the protractor upon A, and the isometrical diameter AB upon AN in the drawing, and above AN describe the curve *i n* between the 15th degree and the point B at zero or nothing. Having removed the protractor draw right line A*i*, and from the point A with the distance of 280 chains cut AN at *h*. Join *i n* and draw *h*B parallel to *n i*, meeting A*i* at B; then AB will represent a distance of 280 chains bearing N 15° W.

Proceed again and draw the right line B*n'* parallel to AN for a new isometrical meridian. Place the centre O of the protractor upon B, and the isometrical diameter AB upon B*n* in the drawing, and below B*n* describe the curve *n'l* between the extremity B at Zero and the 60th degree at *l*. Draw the right line B*l*; from B with the distance of 600 chains cut B*n'* at *k*; draw *k*C parallel to *n'l* meeting B*l* at C, and BC represents a distance of 600 chains bearing N 60° E.

In the same manner, by drawing C*n''* parallel to AN, we shall have the position and length of the line CD and so on.

Ex. 2. Describe isometrically a boundary consisting of ten sides of an enclosed space, the bearings and lengths, successively, of nine sides being respectively N25°E, 150,—N75°E, 200,—S60°E, 100,—direct south 250,—S30°E, 300,—S45°W, 400,—S80°W, 350,—N50°W, 400,—and N20°E, 350.*

* In practical surveying, the bearing of the tenth side would also be taken by the instrument and the distance measured, which being protracted in the usual manner, would be a test of the accuracy of the survey; but in a theoretical point of view, the last line need not be measured, but may be calculated to a greater degree of minuteness than the imperfection of mechanical drawing will admit of; and as an instance of this mode of calculation, an example is annexed of the survey of a space inclosed by right lines, in which the bearing and distance of the last line are not given. When an

Proceed with this example in the same manner as in
the preceding, observing that the meridian **AN** and

enclosure has many sides it is difficult to find the position of the
point between the last line but one and the last line itself. The
best check for this purpose is, to consider every enclosing line
as the hypothenuse of a right-angled triangle, of which one of
the sides containing the right angle is parallel, and the other
perpendicular to the meridian. For if the sides of all the triangles
be found successively and consecutively, the difference between the
sum of all the sides which are parallel to the meridian in the
contrary directions, will show whether the point arrived at is
on the north or south of the point of commencement, and the
difference between the sum of all the sides which are perpendicular to
the meridian in contrary directions will shew whether the point
arrived at is on the east or west side of the meridian, passing through
the point of commencement. The two differences thus found are
evidently the two sides containing the right angle of a right-angled
triangle, of which the hypothenuse is the last side of the figure, and
the two sides are parallel and perpendicular to the meridian. Hence
by the 47th proposition of Euclid, the length of the last side may be
ascertained, and the bearing will be found by trigonometry. The
methods for computing the sides of these triangles are as follows.
The general name of the side of every triangle in the meridian, or
parallel thereto, is called *the difference of latitude*, and the general
name of the side of every triangle which is perpendicular to the meridian is called *the departure.*

It will be necessary to observe, that in making such a survey a
meridian is supposed to pass through the extremity we first arrive at of
every line in our progress of going round ; this point is called the point
of observation. The difference of latitude if north of the point of observation is called *a northing*, if south of the point of observation is called
*a southing*; and the departure if east of the meridian is called an
*easting*, and west a *westing*. The angle at the point of observation is
called *the bearing*, and the hypothenuse of the triangle is called *the
distance.*

The sides of these triangles may be found by a table of the difference of latitude and departure, such as are generally inserted in books

its parallels are right hand lines; and, therefore, the isometrical diameter AB is applied as in the preceding

.of navigation; or if such tables are not at hand, or are not sufficiently extensive, we must have recourse to trigonometry and logarithms, as follows:—

1st. log. diff. lat. = log. cos. bearing + log. distance—10.

2nd. log. departure = log. sin. bearing + log. distance—10.

To apply these two theorems in finding the difference of latitude and departure of the first side of the figure of which side the bearing is N. 25° E., and the distance 150. In each of these theorems for bearing substitute 25°, and for distance substitute 150, and they become

log. diff. lat. = log. cos. 25° + log. 150—10.

log. departure = log. sin. 25° + log. 150—10.

Hence by a table of logarithms find the sine and cosine of 25, and the logarithms of 150; and substitute these values respectively, for sine 25°, cos. 25°, and 150 in the two last equations; and we have

log. diff. lat. = 9·057276 + 2·176091 — 10 = 2·133367 = log. 135·9

and log. dep. = 9·625948 + 2·176091 — 10 = 1·802039 = log. 63·4

The remaining numbers may be computed in the same manner. The bearings and distances, and the results, are here arranged in the following traverse table in columns under bearings, distances, northings, &c., and the sum of the numbers in each column is placed underneath.

| No. | Bearings. | Dist. | Differences of Lat. | | Departures. | |
|---|---|---|---|---|---|---|
| | | | Northings. | Southings. | Eastings. | Westings. |
| 1 | N. 25° E. | 150 | 135·9 | ...... | 63·4 | ...... |
| 2 | N. 75° E. | 200 | 51·8 | ...... | 193·2 | ...... |
| 3 | S. 60° E. | 100 | ...... | 50·0 | 86·6 | ...... |
| 4 | South. | 250 | ...... | 250·0 | ...... | ...... |
| 5 | S. 30° E. | 300 | ...... | 259·8 | 150·0 | ...... |
| 6 | S. 45° W. | 400 | ...... | 283·5 | ...... | 283·5 |
| 7 | S. 80° W. | 350 | ...... | 60·8 | ...... | 344·7 |
| 8 | N. 50° W. | 400 | 257·2 | ...... | ...... | 306·5 |
| 9 | N. 20° E. | 350 | 328·9 | ...... | 119·7 | ..... |
| | | | 773·8 | 904·1 | 612·9 | 934·7 |
| | | | | 773·8 | | 612·9 |
| | | | | 130·3 | | 321·8 |

example. The inclosure drawn according to the bearings and the measures of its sides are exhibited in Fig. 2 geometrically, and in Fig. 3 isometrically.

Ex. 3. Draw the representation of a rectangular house with a regular hipped roof and a chimney shaft in the centre; the front having a southern aspect, the roof an inclination of 25°, the length of the fron: being 30 feet, the length of the end 18 feet, the height of the wall 14 feet, the height of the chimney above the apex of the roof 3 feet, the breadth 5 feet, and the thickness 2 feet.

Let a Fig. 1, Plate XIV., be the projection of the nearest point of the plan of the building.

Draw a b parallel to the meridian line, SN, draw the isometrical line a c, making an angle with a b to repre-

The differences 130·3 and 321·8 are the sides containing the right angle of the last triangle next to the point of commencement. Hence the hypothenuse of this triangle is equal to the

$$\sqrt{\left\{(130{\cdot}3)^2 + (321{\cdot}8)^2\right\}} = 347{\cdot}1 \text{ the length of the 10th line.}$$

The difference 130·3 below the column under southings, shows the extremity of the 9th side to be 130·3 on the south of the point A of commencement, and the difference 321·8 below the column under westings shows that the same point or extremity is 321·8 on the west side of the meridian passing through the point A. Hence by trigonometry and logarithms we have

log. tan. bear. = log. departure + log. rad. — log. dif. lat. and by substitution

$$\text{log. tan. bear.} = \text{log. } 321{\cdot}8 + 10 - \text{log. } 130{\cdot}3$$
$$= 2{\cdot}507586 + 10 - 2{\cdot}114944$$
$$= 10{\cdot}392642 = \text{log. tan. } 67° \, 58'$$

Hence the bearing and distance of the last line JA is N. 67° 58, E. 347·1.

sent a perpendicular to the meridian (by Prop. XII.) and draw the isometrical line $a\,d$, making an angle with $a\,b$ to represent a right line perpendicular to the horizon (by Prop. XIII.)   Make $a\,c$ equal to 30 feet,* $a\,b$ equal to 18 feet, and $a\,d$ equal to 14 feet.   Complete the parallelograms $a\,d\,e\,c$, $a\,d\,f\,b$, $d\,e\,g\,f$.   Prolong $a\,b$ if necessary to $x$, and make the angle $x\,a\,y$ (by Prop. XV) to represent an angle in a vertical plane of 25°, the inclination of the roof.

In order to represent the part of the chimney above the roof.   Since this part is required to be in the middle, and since its thickness is 2 feet, the distance of each of the faces perpendicular to the front wall from each end or flank will be 14 feet ($=\frac{1}{2}$ (30) — 1); therefore, in $d\,e$ make $d\,h$ equal to 14 feet, and draw $h\,i$ parallel to $d\,f$, meeting $f\,g$ in $i$. In $h\,i$ make $h\,k$ equal to 9 feet, half the breadth of the building. Draw $k\,o$ parallel to $a\,d$, and $h\,l$ parallel to $a\,y$, meeting $k\,o$ in $l$. Join $l\,i$, and $h\,l\,i$ represents the profile of the roof in the plane of the chimney parallel to the end represented by $a\,d\,f\,b$. Through $l$ draw $m\,n$ parallel to $g\,f$ or $e\,d$. Now since the length of the house is 30 feet, and the breadth 18 feet, the length of the ridge is 12 feet ($=30-18$).   Since the point represented by $l$ is one

---

* In order to guard the reader against a misapplication of scales, it will not be superfluous to observe, once for all, that all dimensions are taken from the isometrical scale, unless otherwise mentioned. This scale is invariable.   The dimensions of in-isometrical lines must be taken from an in-isometrical scale, and the dimensions of out-isometrical lines from an out-isometrical scale.   These two scales will vary according to the position of the lines, every one requiring a particular scale of its own.

feet nearer to the end represented by *a d f b* than the middle of the thickness of the chimney, make *l m* equal to 7 feet, and *l n* equal to 5 feet. Draw *m g*, *me,n d*, and *n f*, which will represent the hips. Make *l o* equal to 3 feet, through *o* draw *p q* parallel to *h i*, and make *o p* and *o q* each equal to 2 feet 6 inches, half the breadth of the chimney. Draw *p r* parallel to *m n*, *p u* and *q t* parallel to *o k*, meeting *h l* and *i l* in *u* and *t*. Complete the parallelograms *u p r v*, *r p q s*, and the entire figure is the isometrical delineation of the house.

## PROP. XV.

To draw an out-isometrical line, making an angle at a given point with a given in-isometrical line, to represent a given angle in a vertical plane, and to find any projected distance, as 10, 20, 30, &c., feet, yards, chains, &c., upon the out-isometrical line.

Let *l t*, Fig. 2, Plate XIV, be the given in-isometrical line, and let *l* be the given point.

Draw *l r* parallel to the isometrical meridian SN. Place the isometrical diameter AB of the protractor upon *l r* with the centre O upon *l*, and draw the curve line *r t* (as in Prop. XIV), representing an arc of a circle in a horizontal plane, of which the centre is the point represented by *l*. Next place the diameter CD of the protractor upon the same line *l r*, and the centre O upon *l*, and draw the curve line *r s* (as in Prop. XV), so that this curve may represent an arc of a circle in a vertical plane, of which the centre is the point represented by *l*. Draw the right lines *r t* and *r s*. Draw an isometrical line to represent a perpendicular to the horizontal plane, and draw *s u* parallel to this line, meeting *l r* in *u*, draw *u v* parallel to *r t*, meeting *l t* in *v*, and draw *v w* parallel to *u s*.   Make *v w* equal to *u s*, and join *l w*, and *t l w* is the angle required.*

Join *r s* and *l s*.   Take the length required from the isometrical scale, and set the extent upon *l r* from *l* to *a*, and draw *a b* parallel to *r s*, meeting *l s* in *b*.   Draw *b c* parallel to *s w*, meeting *l w* in *c*, and *l c* is the dis-ance required.

## EXAMPLE.

Draw the representation of a house the same in all respects as that described in page 108, except in regard of the aspect, the front being south declining to the west 70 degrees.

In the delineation of the object according to the aspect given, the vertical lines will only be isometrical;

---

* For since *l r* and *l s* are the projections of equal lengths, and since *u s* is the projection of a right line perpendicular to the line represent-ed by *l r*, *l u* is the projection of the cosine, and *s u* the projection of the sine, to the radius of which the projection is *l s*; and since *l r* and *l t* are the projections of equal lengths, any right line parallel to *r t* will cut *l r* and *l t* into distances from *l*, which are the projections of equal lengths ; hence *l u* and *l v* are the projections of equal lengths, and since *l u s* is the projection of a right angle, and since *v w* is equal to *u s*, the right lines *l s* and *l w* are the projections of equal lengths, and the angles *u l s* and *v l w* are the projections of equal angles.

Moreover, because *a b* is parallel to *r s*, the right lines *l a* and *l b* are the projections of equal lengths, and since *l s* and *l w* are the pro-jections of equal lengths, *l b* and *l c* are the projections of equal lengths ; therefore *l c* and *l b* are the projections of equal lengths.

hence the dimensions of the delineation of the plan must be taken from two scales which not only differ from each other, but also from the isometrical scale.

Draw the right line *p r*, Fig. 3, Plate XIV., parallel to the meridian SN, and in *p r* take any convenient point *l*. Place the isometrical diameter AB of the protractor upon *p r*, with the centre O upon *l*, draw the curves *p q, r t*, upon the curve *p q* mark the point *q* at 70 from *p*, and upon the curve *r t* mark the point *t* at 20 (=90—70) from *r*. Join *l q* and *l t*, and draw the chords *p q, r t*. Upon *l r* and *l p* make *l o, l o* each equal to 10, make *l*-10, *l*-10 each equal to 20, and in *l p* make *l*-20 equal to 30. These dimensions being all taken from the isometrical scale R.S. Parallel to *p q* draw 0-0, 10-10, 20-20, &c. meeting *l q* in the points *o*, 10. 20, &c., and parallel to *r t* draw 0-0, 10-10, &c. meeting *l t* in the points 0, 10, &c. Then the lengths of all the in-isometrical lines which represent the right lines that are parallel to each other in the front and roof, and also parallel to the horizon will be found by the scale *l q* to which these lines are parallel, and the lengths of all the in-isometrical lines which represent the right lines that are parallel to each other in the flank and on the roof, and also parallel to the horizon, will be found by the scale *l t* to which these lines are parallel.

Make the angle *t l w* (by Prop. XV.) with the in-isometrical line *l t* to represent an angle in a vertical plane equal to 25°.[*]

[*] The same letters of reference being used as in Proposition.

Let $a$, Fig. 4, be the projection of the nearest point of the plan of the building. Draw $a\,c$ and $a\,b$ respectively parallel to $l\,q$ and $l\,t$, Fig. 3. Make $a\,c$ equal to 30 feet from the scale $l\,q$, Fig. 3, and $a\,b$ equal to 18 feet from the scale $l\,t$, Fig. 3. Draw the isometrical line $a\,d$ to make an angle with $a\,b$, to represent a right line perpendicular to the horizon, and make $a\,d$ equal to 14 feet from the isometrical scale R.S. Complete the parallelograms $a\,d\,e\,c$, $a\,d\,f\,b$, $d\,e\,g\,f$, which represent the faces of the walls. In $d\,e$ make $d\,h$ equal to 14 feet from the scale $l\,q$, Fig. 3. Draw $h\,i$ parallel to $d\,f$, meeting $f\,g$ in $i$, and in $h\,i$ make $h\,k$ equal to 9 feet from the scale $l\,s$, Fig. 3. Draw $k\,o$ parallel to $a\,d$, and $h\,l$ parallel to $l\,w$, Fig. 3, meeting $k\,o$ in $l$. Join $l\,i$. Through $l$ draw $m\,n$ parallel to $g\,f$, make $l\,m$ equal to 7 feet, and $l\,n$ equal to 5 feet, both from the scale $l\,q$, Fig. 3. Draw the right lines $m\,g$, $m\,e$, $n\,d$, $n\,f$. Make $l\,o$ equal to 3 feet from the isometrical scale, and through $o$ draw $p\,q$ parallel to $l\,s$, Fig 3. Draw $u\,v$, $p\,r$, $q\,s$ parallel to $l\,q$, Fig. 3, and make $p\,r$ equal to 2 feet from the scale $l\,q$, Fig. 3. Complete the parallelograms $u\,p\,r\,v$, $q\,p\,r\,s$, and the entire figure is the projection required.

## PROP. XVII.

Given the centre of an ellipse, which is the isometrical projection of a circle, and the isometrical radius of the circle, to describe the ellipse, so that the minor axis may fall upon a given indefinite right line.

Let $o$, Fig. 1, Plate XV., be the given centre, and IJ the given indefinite right line.

H

Through o draw EF perpendicular to IJ. Place the minor axis of the ellipse, forming the surrounding edge of the protractor, upon the given indefinite right line IJ, and the extremities of the major axis upon EF; then upon the drawing mark the extremity of any isometrical diameter at C, and also mark the two extremities of the two axes at E and H with the same letters as are upon the instrument. Remove the protractor, and join the middle point C to each of the two extreme points E and H. Draw two right lines oC and oE. From the centre o with the given isometrical radius cut oC at k, and through k draw k l parallel to CE, meeting oE in l, and draw k m parallel to CH, meeting oH in m. Prolong m o to p, and l o to n. Make o n equal to o l, and o p equal to o m. Upon the two axes l n and p m describe the ellipse l m n p, which is the projection of the circle required.

EXAMPLE.

Let it be required to describe an ellipse, which shall be the isometrical projection of a circle 10 feet diameter, upon a given centre, and its minor axis upon a given indefinite right line.

Proceed with the instrument as before, and having removed it, make o k equal to 5 feet. Draw k l parallel to CE, meeting o E in l, and draw k m parallel to CH, meeting o I in m. Prolong l o to n, and m o to p. Make o p equal to o m, o n equal to o l. Upon the two axes l n, m p, describe the ellipse l m n p, which is the projection of the circle.

Fig. 2, Plate XV., exhibits the method of delineating

the isometrical protractor, which has been fully and generally described (in pages from 97 to 100), without reference to a diagram.  BCDE is the isometrical square, each of its sides BC, CD, DE, EB, are double lines of tangents, each half containing the tagent of 45°, the points $e$, $f$, $g$, $h$, bisecting the four sides of the square, being zero, or the points in which the tangents upon each side begin.  The protractor is exhibited within the isometrical square.  Both have the same common centre. Though a well-divided scale has been recommended, we have here exhibited a complete geometrical construction, which shews how such lines are divided.

Thus from the centre $e$ of the side BE of the isometrical square, draw $e$ A perpendicular to this same side BE, and make $e$ A equal to $e$ B.    From the centre A, with any convenient radius (the larger the better), describe an arc, meeting BA and $e$ A, divide this arc into nine equal parts (which will contain 5° each), and draw right lines from A through the points of division in the arc to meet the right line $e$ B, and thus the half side of the square BE is divided into a line of tangents of 45°. The points of division upon $e$ B are transferred upon $e$ E, and upon $f$ B, $f$ C, $g$ C, $g$ D, $h$ D, $h$ E.   By drawing lines from the points of division on the tangent lines to the centre $s$ of the ellipse, the curved edge will be divided into parts representing five degrees each, as here exhibited.

This method of dividing the line of tangents will become evident by considering that all right lines in orthographical projection are divided in the same proportion as their originals.

### CONCLUDING OBSERVATIONS ON THE METHODS OF DESCRIBING THE CURVE OF AN ELLIPSE.

There is nothing so incommodious to the draughtsman as the description of a correct ellipse. In general,
when it was required to be drawn upon two given axes,
those whose office it was to describe the figure, have
found themselves incompetent to the undertaking, and
have been under the necessity of substituting in its
place an oval compounded of four circular arcs, without attending to the degree of curvature which these
arcs ought to possess, so that the figure thus substituted
wanted that elegance and continuity which are so dis-
tinguishable in the true ellipse, and consequently even
unworthy of being called a representation.

In practice, the mechanic can have recourse to a
trammel by which the curve may be described in the
most perfect manner, by continued motion; or if the
figure be very large, a great number of points at small
distances from each other may be found, and the curve
drawn through these points by the edge of a flexible
lath kept in its place by nails or pins, *as was practised
in the construction of the centres of the New London
Bridge*, by a method first shewn in Nicholson's Carpenter's Guide.

We cannot conveniently apply these methods to
drawing upon paper. Draughtsmen who have a good
eye and a steady hand, may, however, find a sufficient
number of points, and trace the curve through them.
But a more complete method is that which was first

published in the School of Architecture and Engineering* in the year 1828.  The following is a description, and contains the substance of the method there inserted.

## PROPOSITION.

To describe four circular arcs at the extremities of two right lines bisecting each other, which arcs shall make the nearest approach possible to as many certain portions of the curve of an ellipse of which the right lines shall be the axes.

Let AB, Fig. 3, Plate XV, be the greater axis, and DE the less, and let C be the centre.  Draw two right lines OP, OQ, Fig. 4, making any convenient angle POQ with each other.  In OP make Ot equal to the greater semi axis (CA or CB) and Or equal to the less. (CD or CE).  From the centre O describe the arcs r s and tQ, meeting oQ in s and Q.  Join t s, draw QP and r u parallel to t s, meeting OP in P and OQ in u. In Fig. 3 prolong DE on both sides of the longer axis AB to v and w.  Make Dv and Ew each equal to OP, Fig. 4, and make Ax and By Fig. 3, each equal to Ou Fig. 4.  From the centre v, Fig. 3, with the distance vD describe the arc f g, from the centre w with the distance wE describe the arc h i, from the centre x with the distance xA describe the arc k l, and from the centre y with the distance yB describe the arc m n.

---

* To the great disappointment of the public and loss to the author, (Mr. Peter Nicholson,) this work was never completed, owing to the failure of the publishers.  The method above alluded to was contained in the fifth number, which was the last published.

In describing these arcs the operator must observe not to make them exceed 30 degrees, that is not to' exceed 15 degrees on each side of each extremity of each axis. The four arcs *f g, h i, k l, m n,* will touch the ellipse of which the axes are AB, DE, at the points D, E, A, B, and will approach at their extremities nearer to the curve, than any other circular arcs that can be drawn. For either of the circular arcs at the extremities of the minor arcs is entirely without the curve of the ellipse, and either of the other two circular arcs at the extremities of the major axis is entirely within the curve of the ellipse, but they approach so near to the curve that if the radius of the two circular axes at the extremities of the minor axis be diminished, or that of the other two be increased, the circular arcs will still touch the curve at the extremities of the axis, but will pass within it in the one case, and without it in the other, and in both cases will cut it. On the contrary, if the radius of the circular axis at the extremities of the minor axis be greater than *v*D or *w*E, the circular axes *f g* and *h i* will only touch the ellipse at the points D and E, and the extremities *f, g, h, i* will be more remote, and if the radius of the circular arcs at the extremities of the major axis be less than A*x* or B*y,* the circular arcs *k l, m n* will touch the ellipse at the points A and B, and the extremities *k, l, m, n* will be more remote from it than the extremities of the curve described from the radius *x*A and *y*B.

From the properties of the radius of curvature of the ellipse, we shall have *as the semi axis minor is to the semi axis major, so is the semi axis major to the radius of curvature at the extremities of the axis minor, and as the semi-axis major is to the semi-axis minor, so is the semi-axis minor to the radius of curvature at the extremities of the axis major.* Hence if the ellipse be the isometrical projection of a circle, we shall have by these properties, and by the properties of isometrical projection,

$1 : \sqrt{3} :: \sqrt{3} : 3$, which is the radius of curvature at the extremities of the axis minor;

and $\sqrt{3} : 1 :: 1 : \sqrt{\frac{1}{3}} = \frac{1}{3} \sqrt{3}$, which is the radius of curvature at the extremities of the axis major. Hence we may describe the arcs $f g$, $h i$, $k l$, $m n$, without the aid of Fig. 4, by making E$v$ and D$w$ each equal to CD or CE the same axis minor, and by making A$x$ and B$y$ each equal to one-third part of (CA or CB) the semi-axis major.

The distance of the focus is equal to the isometrical radius of the circle.

For in an ellipse which is the isometrical projection of a circle, when the semi-axis major is the $\sqrt{3}$, the semi-axis minor will be 1. Now by the properties of conic sections, the distance of the focus from the centre is the base of a right-angled triangle of which the hypothenuse is the semi-axis major, and the perpendicular the semi-axis minor; hence by the 47th of Euclid, Book first, the square of the base will be equal to the difference of the squares of the hypothenuse and the perpendicular; therefore, if from the point D or E with the semi-axis major (CA or CB) we cut each semi-axis, the points of section $z$, $z'$ will be the two focii; hence if the ellipse be the isometrical projection of a circle, we shall have the hypothenuse equal to the $\sqrt{3}$, and the perpendicular equal to 1 ; therefore, the square of the hypothenuse will be 3, and the square of the perpendicular 1 : hence the difference of these squares is 2 (= 3 — 1) which is the square of the base of the triangle, and therefore the distance of the focus from the centre is also equal to $\sqrt{2}$ the isometrical radius of the circle.

Hence, when the isometrical radius is given, and if we wish to find the focus, we have only to set the isometrical radius from the centre upon each side of it, and upon the axis major, and each point of distance will be the focus.

Again, from the properties of conic sections, the *latus rectum, which is an ordinate to the ellipse at each focus, is a third proportional to the semi-axis major and the semi-axis minor ;* hence the latus rectum is equal to $\frac{1}{2}\sqrt{3}$ ; hence, if through the points $z$ and $z'$, we draw the right lines $\gamma\gamma'$, $\delta\delta'$ and make $z\gamma$, $z\gamma'$, $z'\delta$, $z'\delta'$ each equal to A$x$ or B$y$, the points $\gamma$, $\gamma'$, $\delta$, $\delta'$ will be in the curve, and if the isometrical radii be given, we shall have four other points in the entire curve, and thus we have two points in each quadrant to describe the part that is wanting by hand. When the whole curve is thus described, we shall have a figure which is a very near approach to the ellipse, and which may therefore represent the isometrical projection of the circle upon paper.

Either semi-axis of the ellipse inscribed in the rhombus is the hypothenuse of a right-angled triangle, of which each of the two legs is one-fourth of the diagonal upon which that semi-axis is placed.

By means of this property, either of the two semi-

axis may be instantly found. Having drawn a right
angle, set one fourth (say of the shorter diagonal) from
the vertex upon each side or leg containing the angle,
transfer the distance between the points of extension
upòn the same diagonal (which we have here supposed
to be the shorter) from the centre towards each extremity, and the distance between these two points is the
axis required.

A clear understanding of the three principal directions of isometrical lines, the measurement of angles,
and the true position of circles in isometrical projection, must be the first object of the student's attention.
In the present chapter, the principles and practical
application of this projection have been elucidated by
numerous examples, the consideration of which will
enable an artist to apply isometrical drawing to any
objects, however complex. Its application to surveys
on a large scale is altogether new, and the union of
horizontal and vertical planes is represented with a
pictorial beauty and geometrical accuracy, which render its principles and practice deserving of attention
from all who would excel in the art of designing
objects, whether for practical utility or for elegant
amusement.

# CHAPTER III.

---

## ISOMETRICAL DRAWING.

---

WHEN any one of the sides of a cube is drawn by *orthographic projection*, on a plane parallel to that side, it appears in its *true geometrical shape*, all the lines being in their true relative position, and all the angles of the picture exactly corresponding with the angles of the original figure. Such, however, as has already been explained, is not the case in perspective drawings, and it now becomes necessary to call particular attention to the form of objects which isometrical projection presents. If a cube of 3 feet be drawn isometrically, every side of the *isometrical cube* will be 2·449 feet; that is, they will be in the ratio to the originals of $\sqrt{2}$ to $\sqrt{3}$ if drawn by the rules of projection, or, in other words, if drawn as such a cube would actually appear, to an eye placed at an infinite distance, and endued with perfect vision. It is doubtless this result of the laws of projection which has long prevented its application to the ordinary purposes of plans and sections, for as the measurement of the objects represented would require a constant enlargement according to this ratio, it would necessarily become so abstruse and complicated as to be unfit for practical purposes.

Ordinary projection supposes the objects to be drawn as they actually appear on a plane interposed between the objects and the eye, and many highly-ingenious rules are founded on this supposition. But though in a geometrical sense this interposition of a plane is the only mode of elucidating the theory and practice of isometrical projection, yet for the practical purposes of plans and sections I consider that it may be altogether kept out of consideration, as tending only to embarrass an artist in its general application. Nor are the isometrical plans or sections described in the present work either projections or perspective representations of the objects delineated in a strict geometrical sense, for if they were, they would be liable to the complicated difficuties, already alluded to.

The *true isometrical projection* of a house or any other object, would require a scale different from that which measures the common *ground plan* or *vertical section* of the same object, and the process of geometrical projection, however simple when regular bodies are to be represented,

would be a work of infinite labour when applied
to the numerous and complicated lines of an
architectural design, or a land or mineral survey.
But since (as appears by the demonstrations in
the preceding chapter) isometrical figures are
proportional in all their directions, the drawing
may be enlarged so much as to admit of the application of the same scale which applies to the
orthographic representation.    This will be readily
understood by referring to Plate VIII., in which
the strict *isometrical projection* of the line AB,
Fig. 1, is the distance $b\ i$, Fig. 4, and the isometrical cube $h\ i\ k\ l\ m\ n$, Fig. 4, is the true projection of the cube of ABCD, Fig. 1.    The
larger cube $a\ f\ c$, Fig. 4, is in all respects proportional to the included projection $i\ l\ n$, and it
is enlarged so that each of its sides may exactly
correspond in length with the orthographic drawings of the same cube in Figures 1, 2, and 3.
Hence in the preceding demonstrations, *isometrical projection* has been considered in a strict
geometrical sense ; but in this and subsequent
chapters, the terms *isometrical drawing* and *planning* will be substituted for *projection*, and by
*isometrical plans, drawings, and sections*, are to
be understood, not the geometrical projection of
the objects, but such a proportional enlargement
of the same as to admit of the application of a

scale in the same manner as to a common ground plan and section of the same objects.

While, therefore, the geometrical *principles of projection* form the foundation for the practice of *isometrical drawing*, the latter, as here elucidated, (though strictly in consonance with pure geometry so far as practical accuracy is concerned), is dependent on the former only so far as it is connected with it by being proportional to it, and it necessarily follows, that if the *true projection* of any object gives a true representation, the *isometrical drawing or plan* on a larger scale, being exactly proportional to the projected representation, must also be correct.

In a common ground plan or section, the paper on which the drawing is made is considered to be the plane on which the objects are situated; but when, as in isometrical plans, a number of different planes are to be shown upon one surface, it becomes necessary to have a representation of some common plane or base to which all the other lines or surfaces may be referred. For geological and mining plans, a horizontal plane or base is the most convenient mode of reference; and from what has been said, it will be easily understood that this plane will appear on paper in the same manner as the upper surface of the isometrical cube, Fig. 7, Plate XII., and that all objects per-

pendicular to this plane will be represented by
lines parallel to those which represent the vertical
sides of the cube in the same figure.   In order to
define this horizontal plane on paper, certain
divisions or lines must be drawn, and isometrical
squares are the most convenient for this purpose,
and are very easily made, the isometrical lines
being found on the centre of the plan as follows.

Assume the point *b*, Fig. 4, to be a convenient
place for the centre of the intended isometrical
drawing, and describe a circle, it matters not with
what radius.   Draw a diameter at right angles
with the top or bottom of the paper, which in the
present instance will be the line *d f.*   From either
extremity of this diameter with the radius of the
circle step the circumference, which gives the
points *a, e, f, g, c,* and when the points are connected by straight lines with each other and with
the centre, an isometrical cube is complete.*   Now
if the cube is required to be of any given size,
the length of one side may form the radius of the
circle; or, which is the same thing, if any radius
be taken, the isometrical lines can be drawn by it,

---

* The straight lines represent the edges which would be
visible if the cube were opake, and the dotted lines *b d, b e,*
*b g,* show the further edges which would also appear if the
cube were perfectly transparent.

and the dimensions set off on the radii of the hexagon ; the outlines of the cube being thus formed, it is obvious that *a b c d* represents the upper surface, *a e f b* and *b f g c* represent the two conterminous sides of *a b* and *b c*, the former being *a horizontal isometrical square,* and the latter *two vertical isometrical squares.* I have ventured to incur the risk of being considered unnecessarily minute in this example, by explanations which to those conversant with geometry are altogether unnecessary : the construction of such an isometrical cube, together with the delineation of objects on it, is, indeed, so extremely simple, that most persons will at once understand it by referring to the figure in Plate 8. But when it is considered that this method of projection is very little known, and scarcely at all practised, and when it is also considered that this problem, simple as it is, is that on which the whole system of isometrical projection entirely depends, I trust to escape censure for endeavouring so to describe it, that every one who knows the first rudiments of geometry may clearly understand its application ; and that whoever understands how to draw a circle and a straight line, may, by very little attention, acquire a familiar knowledge of this construction, which may be considered the foundation of isometrical drawing. This problem, also, is

equally a foundation for the construction of plans
of buildings and machinery; and it must be kept
in mind, that there are many enquiring and ingenious persons in various departments of life, who
are deterred from scientific pursuits by the cloud
of mystery which too often invests the explanation
of such subjects, and, even in such examples as
the present, might be deterred, by considering the
matter one of greater difficulty than it really is :
and though the distinctions between strict isometrical projection and that here suggested for practical use, may not at first be perfectly understood
by every one, yet all the practical part may be
just as well pursued without any knowledge of
these distinctions.   To those unaccustomed to
geometry, it would be a most elaborate task to
elucidate, in a familiar manner, all the principles
and methods of true isometrical projection ; but
I trust enough has been said to enable any one,
with a pair of common compasses, to draw an
isometrical cube of any size, or to draw any number of isometrical squares, adjoining each other,
and all similar in *form and position* to that which
represents the *upper surface* of the cube in Fig.
4, Plate VIII.

In Plate IX, Fig. 1 represents an area of
ground perfectly square and level, and containing
the following objects: a road 20 feet wide, a church

50 feet long and 20 wide, a house 33 feet by 20, with some trees, hedges, walls, and tombstones, all which are delineated on a scale of 100 feet to $1\frac{1}{2}$ inch; and so far as the exact relative size and position of these objects on one plane are concerned, no other mode of planning can ever compete with this for simplicity, and for the convenience of measuring distances in any direction. But if it were required to show also the height of the church and house, the depth of borings, and the strata intersected by them, recourse must be had to vertical sections or elevations, and the two sides A B and B C can only be shown by two separate drawings as at Fig. 2 and 3. In these, the heights, of the church 25 feet, the tower 50 feet, and the house 20 feet, are distinctly shown; and the depths of the borings, viz. No. 1, 10 fathoms, of No. 2, 15 fathoms, of No. 3, 14 fathoms, are also correctly delineated. Hence these separate drawings, viz. *the ground plan, and two sections*, afford a correct idea of the three several planes represented, but each drawing comprehends only the objects which are upon that particular plane. *The ground plan, Fig.* 1, gives no idea of the *heights or depths;* and *the vertical sections, Fig.* 2 *and* 3, give no idea of the *relative area and position of the surface objects.* Fig. 4 represents an isometrical drawing showing

I

all these planes, and as parallel lines have been adopted in this instance, for clearness of illustration, it will be readily seen that by means of a pair of common compasses and a parallel ruler, the lines on No 1 may easily be transferred to Fig. 4 in this manner.

Having drawn the hexagonal representation of the cube Fig. 4, as in Plate VIII, so that each of the sides exactly corresponds in length with the sides of Fig. 1, set off with a common scale the distances along the line $a\ b$, the same as on A B,* and also along the line $b\ c$, mark the termination of the road in like manner, and the position of the house on $c\ d$. Connect the corresponding portions of the roads, &c. by lines drawn parallel to the sides of the isometrical square, and an isometrical ground plan of the road will easily be formed on Fig. 4. Having completed this, the dimensions of the church and house may be set off upon the road lines, and all these objects being parallel to the isometrical lines, admit of being

---

* A very convenient mode of transferring distances from one plan to another is to place a thin piece of paper with a straight edge along one of the lines to be copied, and to mark the several divisions with a fine pencil, by placing the same on the other line, these divisions may be transferred with great facility, and with sufficient accuracy for most practical purposes.

measured by one uniform scale. When the ground plan of the roads, church, and house is obtained, the next object is to delineate their vertical dimensions ; and as all *vertical lines* on isometrical drawings are measured by the same scale as the isometrical lines, this matter is easily accomplished, the walls of the church, for instance, being 25 feet high are drawn so, the tower 50 feet, and the walls and hedges along the roads varying from 4 to 10 feet high. An inspection of the drawing will preclude the necessity of going in detail through the whole minutiæ of the operations, and to many I am aware, the present explanation may already appear too verbose. Having, however, occasionally experienced some difficulty in giving a clear conception of these first principles of isometrical drawing, I am willing to risk the error of being unnecessarily minute, rather than be imperfectly understood. It is not so much by any knowledge of a series of rules that a facility in this mode of drawing can be required, as by a complete knowledge of its first principles. I am therefore anxious to explain these with as much clearness and simplicity as the subject will admit of ; if, however, to any of my readers the present example should not be perfectly intelligible, I would recommend the simple expedient of making a small pasteboard model of a cube, and *drawing*

I 2

on its sides the several features exhibited in Fig.
1, 2, 3, Plate IX.  If through this cube a long
straight wire be projected diagonally, and the eye
placed in this direction, an isometrical view of the
cube will be obtained, and if on the upper surface
small models of the church, house, walls, &c. be
placed, their appearance together with the previous
explanations will afford the most clear and intelligible idea of isometrical drawing, which is simply
the true representation on paper, of objects when
viewed in this direction.

In order to convey a familiar idea of the mode
of applying isometrical drawing to mineral plans
and sections, the sides of the cube, Fig. 4, Plate
IX., are supposed to exhibit the strata and seams
of coal lying under the church and adjacent
ground, as ascertained by borings at Nos. 1, 2,
and 3.   These borings being perpendicular, the
several strata, &c., are drawn by a common scale
upon them, in the same manner as they would be
on common vertical sections, as Figures 2 and 3.
A throw or disruption of the strata by a vein or
dyke, is also represented, in order to shew the
great ease and clearness with which this mode of
drawing may be applied to geological illustrations,
as well as to the representation of buildings and
other objects on the surface.   As this imaginary
instance of a cube, however, is one which pos-

sesses a degree of simplicity rarely to be expected
in delineating plans and sections, it is necessary
to consider the difficulties which may occur in
applying isometrical drawing to more complicated
objects.   In order to do this with greater clearness and precision, the reader is referred to the
definitions at page 96, which, together with the
accompanying demonstrations and rules, will enable the geometrical student to pursue the subject
with ease and facility.    A brief recapitulation of
some of these rules and definitions may, however,
be introduced for the use of the general reader,
and a familiar explanation of them afforded by the
isometrical drawing which has just been described.

In Fig. 4, Plate IX., *ab, bc, cd, da, ae, ef
fg, gc,* and all lines parallel to any of these, are
ISOMETRICAL LINES, the edges *ab, bf,* and *bc,* are
CONTERMINOUS EDGES of the cube, and the three
sides which are presented to view are CONTERMI-
NOUS FACES.   In Plate VIII., the lines *ab, bc,* in
Fig. 4, represent the ISOMETRICAL DRAWING OR
PLAN of the lines AB, BC, Fig. 1, drawn, not as
they would appear by true projection, as at *ib, bn,*
but enlarged so that each side of the isometrical
cube is equal to the corresponding sides represented, and consequently may be measured by the
same scale as a common ground plan and section.
In other words, the isometrical length of 3 feet,

*by projection,* is 2·449 feet, but in the practical application of this mode of drawing to plans and sections, as here elucidated, the dimensions on the isometrical lines exactly coincide with the dimensions of the object represented.

IN-ISOMETRICAL LINES are right lines drawn on, or parallel to, any of the conterminous faces of a cube, but not parallel to any of the edges; thus the dykes or veins *vv, vv,* Fig. 4, Plate IX., are represented by in-isometrical lines.

OUT-ISOMETRICAL LINES are right lines which are neither contained on the faces of the cube, nor are parallel to them or to any of the edges of an isometrical cube; thus the trunk of the tree *t,* in Fig. 4, Plate IX., is an out-isometrical line.

ISOMETRICAL ANGLES represent the projection of a right angle, and are either 60° or 120°: *abf, bfe,* and *fea,* Fig. 4, Plate IX., are isometrical angles.

IN-ISOMETRICAL ANGLES are angles in any of the conterminous faces of a cube, or in planes parallel to them; thus *vvg, vve,* are in-isometrical angles. The trunk of the tree *t* Fig. 4, Plate IX, is an OUT-ISOMETRICAL ANGLE.

The right hand and left hand isometrical lines will be readily understood by inspecting Fig. 4, Plate IX., in which *bc* and *fg,* are *right hand lines ; ba* and *fe* are *left hand lines : gc,* in the same figure, is a right hand vertical line, and *ea* a left hand vertical line.

The above are definitions without which it would be difficult to describe the application of isometrical drawing to several of the subsequent examples ; and it is desirable that every one who, either for utility or amusement, proposes to practice it, should clearly comprehend them. The student who would be master of the subject will also do well to go carefully through the several demonstrations and problems in the preceding chapter, and to construct the examples there given.

As the whole system of isometrical drawing is dependent on the lines of the isometrical cube, which form the basis both for constructing the drawings, and for obtaining the dimensions, it is desirable to possess every facility for the construction of these base lines which require to be so frequently drawn and referred to. For this purpose, Professor Farish recommends what may be called an isometrical T square or bevel,* which

* " There should be a ruler in the form of the letter T to slide on one side of the drawing-table. The ruler should be kept, by small prominences on the under side, from being in immediate contact with the paper, to prevent its blotting the fresh drawn lines as it slides over them. And a second ruler, by means of a groove near one end on its under side,

is described in the note.   In order to use this T square or level, the paper is required to be stretched on a drawing board or table, and the instrument itself not only requires very great care in its construction, but the sliding grove is liable to become incorrect by use.   The triangular rulers described in the following section answer all the purposes of isometrical drawing in a simple and rapid manner, and have the advantage of projecting the vertical as well as the right and left hand

should be made to slide on the first.   The groove should be wider than the breadth of the first ruler, and so fitted, that the second may at pleasure be put into either of the two positions represented in the plate, Fig. 1, Plate XVII, so as to contan with the former ruler, in either position, an angle of 60 degrees.   The groove should be of such a size, that when its shoulders *a* and *d* are in contact with, and rest against the edges of the first ruler, the edge of the second ruler should coincide with *d e*, the side of an equilateral triangle described on *d g*, a portion of the edge of the first ruler; and when the shoulders *b* and *c* rest against the edges of the first ruler, the edge of the second should lie along *g e*, the other side of the equilateral triangle.   The second ruler should have a little foot at *k* for the same purpose as the prominences on the first ruler, and both of them should have their edges divided into inches, and tenths, or eighths of inches. It would be convenient if the second ruler had also another groove *r s*, so formed that when the shoulders *r* and *s* are in contact with the edges of the first ruler, the second should be at right angles to it."

*Professor Farish's Paper on Isomet. Perspective.*

isometrical lines.   They may be rendered useful
for many geometrical problems, as the construction
of triangles and of rectangular figures; they are also
adapted for two very effective modes of delineating objects, by combining an orthographic drawing of one plane, with a species of isometrical projection of other two sides :  they at the same time
possess all the usefulness of the German parallel
rulers, may be used on any paper without being
stretched, and have also the desirable qualifica-
tions of cheapness and portability.

## DESCRIPTION AND USE OF THE PROJECTING AND PARALLEL RULERS INVENTED BY T. SOPWITH.

In every mode of drawing where precision is
required, the aid of instruments is indispensable.
In ordinary landscape drawing, a skilful artist can
represent straight or curved lines of every description, with sufficient accuracy to convey a general
idea of the picturesque appearance of objects; and
by practice, some persons have acquired great
facility in drawing mathematical figures by the
hand alone, of which the illustrations in Phillips'
Mineralogy are a remarkable example.   But in
all those kinds of drawing which are intended for
practical use and reference, and when parallel
lines, angles, and other definite objects, are to be

shown with geometrical truth, it is necessary to be
provided with such instruments as are most readily
and correctly applied for these respective purposes.   The compasses, protractor, T square,
and parallel rulers are in general use, and suffice
for the delineation of such lines as are most commonly required in mechanical plans and drawings ;
but there are other instruments of great utility
which are much less known, such, for instance, as
the Centrolinead invented by Mr. Nicholson,*
which greatly lessens the difficulty experienced
in drawing lines converging to a distant centre,
and which for making the diminishing lines of
common perspective is exceedingly useful.   Such,
also, are various instruments for the description
of curve lines, as the Multamater invented by
Mr. Hance, Suardi's Geometric pen, Professor
Wallace's Eidograph, together with various improvements of other mathematical instruments.
The triangular scale and ruler, called Marquoi's
parallel scales, and Keith's improvement of
them, are not generally known, though they
afford great facility in the construction of some
geometrical figures ; and the isometrical rulers
recommended by Professor Farish have not, that

* For which ingenious and useful invention Mr. N. received a premium of 20gs., and a silver medal, from the
Society of Arts, April 10th, 1814.

I am aware of, been manufactured for sale.
Different methods of representing objects therefore, admit of being rendered of more easy and
simple application by the aid of particular instruments, and this is a department of art which will
doubtless be found capable of much improvement,
if ever mechanical and geometrical drawing is en-
couraged to an extent commensurate with its vast
utility and importance in a manufacturing and mining country.   In attempting the delineation of
objects by the isometrical mode of drawing, my
attention was directed to some more portable and
convenient method of projecting isometrical lines
than the drawing board and sliding bevel suggested
by Professor Farish, especially as any error in the
shoulder of the latter instrument would be greatly
increased at the further end of the blade.   It
occurred to me that isometrical triangles might be
constructed so as to answer the several purposes
of projecting the principal vertical and horizontal
lines, and at the same time be useful as parallel
rulers and scales.   These have the advantage of
being extremely portable, and may be used on
paper of any size without a drawing board ; they
consist of three triangles represented in Plate XVI.
No. 1 is a right-angled triangle ABC, the angle
A being 60°, and the angle C 30°.   No. 2 is an
isosilis triangle AED, of which the angles A and

D are each 30°, and the angle E consequently is
120°. No. 3, an equilateral triangle CED, each
angle being of course 60°. Now as all the angles
formed by the intersection of isometrical lines are
either 60° or 120°, it will readily appear that these
rulers may be used for the projection of such lines
in any required position, as well as for drawing
parallel lines, in the same manner as Marquoi's
parallel scales, or German parallel ruler. As it is
convenient to have the true form of the isometrical ellipse for representing circular objects, as
wheels, &c., such an ellipse is represented on
each ruler; that on No. 1 is the isometrical drawing of a circle 2 inches in diameter. On No. 2
is a similar ellipse, having the isometrical diameter
1 inch; and on No. 3, the diameter is $1\frac{1}{2}$ inch.*
In ivory scales of this description, it would be
desirable to have these several ellipses cut out, so
that an isometrical circle or wheel could readily _
be drawn round the edge, and the sides AB, DE,
EA, ED, and DC, might also be made with a
fiducial edge, and a graduated scale of tenths.
The cylinder and cube on No. 1 are introduced
as illustrations of this mode of drawing, and the
inscriptions on the top and two sides of the latter

---

* For the method of constructing an isometrical ellipse of
any required dimensions, see pages from 111 to 120.

render it a clear illustration of the principles of isometrical projection.

If the side B C of the triangle No.·1 be placed parallel to the under edge of the sheet of paper on which an isometrical drawing is intended to be made, the edge A C will form what in the preceding demonstrations has been called *a left hand isometrical line*, the meaning of which will be obvious by examining the lettered isometrical cube, and considering that all *isometrical lines on a horizontal plane* are, in fact, lines parallel to the right or left hand sides of a cube viewed isometrically. The edge E C of the ruler No. 3 being then applied to the edge A C of No. 1, the edge E D will form *a right hand isometrical line on a horizontal plane*, and the side D C will be a *vertical line*, parallel of course to the upright edges of the cube. By sliding the edge E C along the edge A C, it is obvious that any number of parallel lines may be drawn by each respective edge, and dimensions in many instances may be set off in the very act of drawing by means of the scales. When left-hand lines are to be drawn above or below the one first drawn along the edge A C, place the edge E C of No. 3 against the edge B C of No. 1, then, by keeping No. 3 firm, and moving No. 1 to the right or left, the several left-hand lines may be drawn in their required positions; or if the plan or drawing is large, a common rectangular ruler may be used in the place of No. 3. In this manner all the principal lines required in isometrical drawing, may be made with great rapidity, and with sufficient accuracy for most practical purposes ; and when it is considered that in buildings, machinery, mines, &c., vertical and horizontal lines are those which most frequently occur, the utility of an easy and convenient mode of delineating them will appear very obvious, while also it is equally evident how great an advantage is afforded by the application of one uniform scale to all these three several directions, a property which distinguishes isometrical drawing from every other mode of projection.

A few attempts to draw an isometrical cube, and afterwards to delineate houses and other objects represented in the plates which accompany this volume, together with the engraved explanations inserted on the rulers, will preclude the necessity of further detailed instructions for their use in isometrical drawing. It may, however, be observed, that they may also be very readily applied to the *division of lines* either into equal or unequal parts, thus :—let it be required to divide the line *a b*, Fig. 2, Plate XVII, into 10·25 parts ; set off from the point *b* a right line *b c* in any convenient direction, and mark on it 10¼ divisions

by *any scale* of equal parts ;  place the edge A C
of the ruler No. 1 so as to coincide with the points
*c* and *a* ;  hold the ruler firmly in this position, and
place any side of the ruler No. 2 against the edge
B C ;  then,  keeping No. 2 steadily in its place,
slide the ruler No. 1 to the right hand, and as the
edge A C intersects the several marks or divisions
on the line *c b*,  mark with a very fine point the
corresponding intersections on the line *a b*, which
will be the required divisions.    This operation is
one which has frequently to be performed in the
construction of isometrical plans, and not only
does it save much time,  but  enables the artist to
avail himself of the  most perfect scales he may
have in his possession.

By sliding the edge D A of No. 2 along the
edge A C of No. 1, a vertical line may be divided into parts which shall be exactly half the
dimensions marked on the scale A C.   Other
uses of these rulers, such as erecting perpendiculars from any part of a given right line, or letting
fall a perpendicular from any given point to a right
line, will readily suggest themselves in the course
of using them, and the same remark may be
made of them which accompanies the description
of Marquoi's parallel scales, viz., that "they answer
every purpose of a pleasant parallel ruler, including
the great advantage of erecting perpendiculars to

any part of a given line, precluding in a great measure the use of the compasses by drawing lines parallel at any required distance ; and consequently most plans, particularly those of fortifications, may be drawn with uncommon accuracy in half the usual time."

The projecting and parallel rulers here described, may be applied, not only to ordinary orthographic projection, but also to two other modes of projection which will frequently be found extremely useful in the delineation of objects, and which also possess the advantage of exhibiting three sides of a rectangular solid, and admitting of the application of the same scale to every side ; and though neither of these methods is applicable to the delineation of large surveys, where bearings are required, yet for many representations of buildings, machines, and details of architectural or engineering objects, they will be found extremely convenient and useful. They both exhibit an orthographical view or elevation of the front side; one of them showing a full view of the upper surface, and a diminished view of one of the sides of a cube, and the other showing a full view of one of the sides, with a diminished view of the surface; the former, therefore, may be called verti-horizontal drawing, and the latter verti-lateral drawing. The construction of these projections of rectangular figures, by means of the ruler No. 1, will easily be understood by referring to the diagrams in Plate XVII.   The edges C B, B A, of No. 1, Fig. 13, being placed in a convenient situation for drawing two sides of a square, the ruler No. 2, or, in its stead, a common rectangular ruler, or straight edge, Z Z, is to be placed against the edge C A of No. 1.   Any given dimensions may then be set off on the edges C B, B A, and any number of parallel lines drawn in each direction, by sliding the ruler No. 1 to the right or left, as at *cb*, *ba*, *b'a,* ; and in this manner these rulers will be found extremely useful in delineating ordinary ground plans and elevations. The orthographic representation of the front of the object being thus completed, the ruler No. 2, or straight edge, is still to be kept firmly in the same position, and if it is required to show the upper surface more than the other vertical side, the shortest side of the ruler No. 1 is to be placed against the ruler No. 2, or straight edge, with the side B C to the left hand, as at X, and the lines *xx x'x'*, drawn by sliding No. 1 along the straight edge ; but if it is desired to show the other vertical side in preference to the surface, then the edge A C of No. 1 is to be kept to the left hand, as at Y, and the lines *yy*, *y'y'*, drawn in like manner; then upon the several lines thus drawn, dimensions

K

may be set off by the same scale which is used in delineating the front view or elevation of the object.

As a further illustration of the drawings produced by means of these rulers, a house is represented by each of the three methods which have been described, in Figures 3, 4, 5, Plate XVII. Fig. 3 is an isometrical drawing of a house, showing the front and end, and accompanied with a view of the arrangement and thickness of the interior walls of the ground floor in Fig. 6. Figs. 4 and 7 are verti-horizontal drawings, and Figs. 5 and 8 are verti-lateral drawings of the same objects. The representation afforded by Fig. 7 is well adapted for giving a clear idea of the several parts of a building, since it not only gives a true elevation of the principal front, but also a very complete view of the interior; while for designs of furniture, the effect produced by the verti-lateral drawing Fig. 11 is extremely convenient. It may be observed, that by reversing the position of the rulers, the opposite sides of the figures may be drawn in like manner, and the under surface also may be represented instead of the upper.

When once a clear conception of the principles of the isometrical lines is obtained, together with a tolerable facility in the construction of simple rectangular figures, it will require some degree of

attention to comprehend the manner in which
these lines are made subservient to the representation and subsequent admeasurement of irregular figures.    It has already been observed, that
where objects are entirely situated on one plane,
no possible mode of drawing is at all comparable
with parallel projection as generally used in
ground plans and elevations.    But wherever the
objects are in planes more or less inclined to
each other, it is utterly impossible to represent the
several dimensions of every part of each on any
plane surface, such as a sheet of paper; and this ·
imperfection, existing of necessity in every mode
of representation, is of course to be found in isometrical drawing.    A ground plan, or an elevation representing *one plane* only, distorts the
dimension of every line not parallel to that plane ;
while an isometrical plan, representing *three planes*
coinciding with the top and two sides of a cube,
distorts the dimensions of all lines not parallel to
the edge of one or other of these three planes,
and hence dimensions can only be measured by
one common scale in isometrical directions.    This
to the learner is at first attended with some perplexity, but it will cease to be so when the nature of geometrical projection is considered ; nor
does it in reality create much difficulty, since
the distortion in every part of the plan admits of

an easy adjustment or admeasurement by isometrical lines. The laws of vision place certain
limits to the means of delineating objects, but
this facility of projection and admeasurement renders isometrical drawing greatly superior to common perspective, both for simplicity and extensive
practical use; the principal lines and angles, being
invariable, may be projected in an easy and rapid
manner, while the art of perspective, as commonly
elucidated, requires long practice, and considerable
geometrical skill. Having, therefore, described
the general principles of isometrical drawing, in
the subsequent chapters it will be endeavoured
to show in what manner, and to what extent,
it may be conveniently used in the representation
of various objects.

# CHAPTER IV.

## APPLICATION OF ISOMETRICAL DRAWING TO GEOLOGY AND MINING.

THE increasing interest of geology, as a subject of general information, forms a prominent feature of the science and literature of the present day, and after being almost entirely neglected for ages, it has obtained a share of attention commensurate with its vast importance. The absurd conjectures and baseless theories which formerly supplied the place of facts and observation, are now consigned to the oblivion they so justly merit; and by geology we understand the study of those phenomena which are presented to our view, and from which it is the province of science to draw such conclusions only as are strictly conformable to reason and experience. " Much importance must be attached to this study by every one who considers how much the well-being both of individuals and of nations depends on the improvement of every means, whether of knowledge or power, committed to our trust. In this country, where so much depends on the mineral products of the earth, too much attention cannot be given to a science so immediately connected with interests so important, and it is gratifying to perceive how rapidly a taste for this and similar departments of science has lately increased. As to the precise period or operation of geological changes, mere theoretical discussions can lead to little or no practical use. Instead, therefore, of idle disputes on Neptunian and Plutonist dreams, let future researches be confined to the collection of carefully-observed facts. When these have been accumulated by industry, and greatly increased by time, some Newton in geology may discover important and general laws guiding the successive changes of the strata. In the meantime, we may rest assured, that records of a patient and constant attention to actually-existing phenomena are the most valuable additions which at this period can be made to the science of geology."*

Drawing is one of the most useful and interesting aids of every art and science, but in no instance is it of so much importance as in recording the facts of geology and mining. The astronomer has frequent opportunities of examining the orbs

* Account of the Mining Districts of Alston Moor, Weardale, and Teesdale, by T. Sopwith.

of heaven,—the botanist has ever a fresh succession of the beauties of vegetation—but while the canopy of heaven and the surface of the earth not only remain open to continued investigation, but are also the common objects of observation to every one, the geologist has to contend with phenomena, many of which can only be seen under peculiar circumstances; and many, which, as in the interior of abandoned mines, are, after a brief period, closed for ever from human observation. The telescope or microscope can afford to every eye a more perfect idea of the appearance of the planets, and of vegetable structure, than any drawings, however perfect; but neither instruments nor descriptions of any kind, can possibly convey so clear and accurate an idea of the geological structure of a mine or district, as that which is given by plans and drawings, which are thus rendered not only *the most important,* but in many cases *the only means* of recording geological facts and observations.

The kind of drawing universally adopted for representing the interior of mines, and the vertical surfaces of real or supposed sections of strata, is that which supposes the eye of the observer to be placed in a direction exactly perpendicular to every part of the plane represented, or in other words, the *ground plan* and *section* which are so

familiar to every one who is conversant either
with the practice of mining or the study of geology.
Plate VI. exhibits a ground plan of a portion of
a lead mine, with a vertical section of the same,
having the representation strictly limited to such
workings and strata as are really known to exist,
and rejecting all supposititious lines of strata, with
which sections are generally too much encumbered.

Now if the adits 1, 2, and 3, in the plan, were
exactly situated on one plane, nothing could afford
a more clear and intelligible idea of their relative
position than the mode in which they are here
drawn.   But the adit, No. 2, is from $3\frac{1}{2}$ to 8
fathoms lower than No. 1, and the cross-cut or
gallery, No. 3, is midway between Nos. 1 and 2,
which vertical position cannot by any possibility
be shown on the ground plan: all that can be done
is to distinguish them by different colours or lines,
to intimate that some difference does exist in
their respective levels, the only explanation of
which can be given, so far as drawing is concerned, by the vertical section.   The eye which, in
viewing the ground plan, was supposed to be
placed directly above the objects represented, is, in
regard to the section, presumed to be at one side;
and hence the several adits are distinctly seen in
their respective elevations, together with the
various strata in which they are driven.   The

same remark applies to the section, which has been made to the ground plan, viz. that if the several objects represented on it were exactly on one plane, then it would form a true geometrical representation of the workings.   But the adit No. 1, instead of being on one, is on no less than nine different planes, and hence a considerable discrepancy arises between the dimensions on the plan and section ; thus, for instance, the true distance from G to H on the plan is 25½ fathoms, but the apparent distance, as given by the usual method of drawing sections, is only 19 fathoms. In some instances it may be convenient to avoid this, by extending the section so as to correspond with the true length, which in the present instance would be done by representing H at *i;* but even this would not give the true length of the adit No. 2, which, notwithstanding its circuitous course from G to H, could only be drawn on the section as though it were as straight as the adit No. 1.   Hence it is to be understood, that the *ground plan* furnishes a geometrical plan of *those objects only* which are *on, or parallel to, a horizontal plane*, and the *section*, as commonly understood, represents *the true dimensions of those objects only* which are *upon, or parallel with, a vertical plane;* and these two drawings cannot be truly combined in one, but form a separate plan and section.

The representation of solid objects on a flat surface is a great achievement of human art, and whoever attentively considers the subject, so far from being surprised that some difficulties occasionally occur, will rather be disposed to admire the very comprehensive idea which is afforded of vast and complicated objects, by means so apparently inadequate.

It is much to be regretted that so little attention has been paid in this country to geometrical drawing, a department of art closely allied to some of the most important interests of the empire. Topographical modelling is scarcely either known or practised;* and when it is considered what

* The author has in his possession a beautiful and interesting model of France, by Schuster, of Dresden, tinted with the deep blue of ocean, the valleys and champaigne countries of the Seine, the Loire, and Garonne, are coloured green, while the high summits of the Alps and Pyrenean Mountains, touched with white, indicate the limit of perpetual snow. It was brought from the continent by Professor Pillans, of Edinburgh, whose attention, in passing along the streets of Dresden, was attracted by the extraordinary merit of this production. The artist who constructed it expressed his desire to undertake a similar model of Great Britain, if due encouragement appeared for such a work. That the English are not wanting in liberal patronage to foreign artists, is sufficiently known to all who have heard of the strains of

extravagant sums are daily expended in mere trifles, it is surprising that a pursuit combining so much elegant amusement with practical science and utility, should be almost utterly neglected. As closely connected with the subject of the present work, I may here take the opportunity of describing a method of constructing models of districts, which combines great accuracy with a constant facility of inspecting every portion of them, and also furnishes one of the most intelligible explanations of the mode of representing the geological structure of a country by isometrical drawing.

The square ABCD, Fig. 1, Plate XVIII., represents a portion of a mining district, one mile in extent, and divided into 64 equal parts by parallel lines a furlong distant from each other. Fig. 2 represents the section over each of the lines parallel to AB, and Fig. 3 comprises the

Catalani, or the fiddle of Paganini. Even foreign modellers have found encouragement in making figures and artificial flowers, &c. in wax; but, without any desire to condemn attention to merit of whatever kind, it may be observed, that works of usefulness ought at least to command an equal share of public favour; and an increasing taste for geology may probably introduce topographical modelling as a favourite and fashionable object of that attention to which its utility and beauty so justly entitle it.

series of sections over the lines parallel to A C.
It is to be observed that, owing to the smallness
of the plate, these figures are here delineated by a
very minute scale, viz. 40 chains or $\frac{1}{2}$ a mile to
1 inch; the vertical sections in Figs. 2 and 3,
are, however, exactly drawn to a proportionate
scale, and therefore give a correct idea of the
relative magnitudes.    Thus the section No. 1 is
100 yards high at A, 180 yards at $b$, and 150
yards at C.  These several sections being cut out
in pasteboard covered with drawing paper, or, what
would be much better, in thin plates of copper,
so prepared with a covering of paint as to admit
of being drawn upon with ink and colours, are to
be joined crossways by what is termed *half-lapping*,
that is, by cutting each section half way down
where it crosses another section cut in like manner on the other edge, as at Fig. 5, and the whole
being properly painted with sections, and joined
together in this manner, as represented in Fig. 4,
will afford an interior view of the geological structure of the district.    The model of squares thus
formed is to be placed on a plane surface, and
the several spaces may be filled with pieces of
wood or Paris plaster, carved or moulded on
the upper surface so as to represent the surface
of the earth; the several slips on which the sections are drawn may at any time be taken out for

examination, or for delineating any new discoveries upon them.

It will readily be perceived that whatever is
known of the geological structure of a district,
whether by the bassetting or cropping out of
strata, the working of quarries, or the sinking of
shafts, and various mining operations, may easily
be drawn on sections corresponding to those
at Figs. 2 and 3, Plate XVIII., but of course
on a considerably larger scale. The isometrical
representation, Fig. 4, may be very readily constructed by means of the rulers described in the
preceding chapter, or set off with a pair of common compasses. From a centre C, Fig. 4, Plate
XVIII., with the radius CA measured from Fig.
1, describe an arc ABD, on which, with the same
radius, the points A and D are set off from B,
the extremity of the vertical radius CB. All
the sections in the isometrical drawing being parallel to the sides, are, by the problem, equal in
length to the lines in Fig. 1, or the sections in
Figs. 2 and 3, and consequently distances may be
delineated or measured upon them by a common
scale. Fig. 6 exhibits a portion of a common
vertical section, and its corresponding isometrical
section. From E to F is a horizontal distance of
4 chains and 40 links, which length is represented
on the isometrical drawing at *e f*. The vertical

heights at E, F, and G, are set off in the isometrical section at *e f g*, as are also the depth of
the shaft at F, and the thickness and inclination of the strata intersected.    In the common
drawing, EG represents a level or a horizontal
line, and the line *e g*, in the isometrical drawing,
also represents a left-hand horizontal line, and
though its apparent obliquity at first seems a
departure from geometrical truth, yet it is founded as well on the strictest geometrical principles
as on the actual appearance of objects, when
viewed in the oblique direction which isometrical
drawing supposes.    We have seen that the common ground plan and section are each limited to
*one plane*, which must form a separate drawing,
while, in the example before us, in Fig. 4, Plate
XVIII., we have *three several planes combined
in one drawing*, all of which can be truly delineated, or afterwards measured by a common scale
applied in the isometrical directions, that is, in
lines parallel to those which represent the edges
of a cube isometrically, as explained in page 126.
Consequently, the plan, Fig. 1, and the sections
in Figs. 2 and 3, which form 19 separate and unconnected drawings, are all united in their true
relative position in one drawing in Fig. 4.

From this great facility in measuring lines
which are upon, or parallel to, isometrical lines, it

obviously follows that, in constructing isometrical drawings and sections, it is desirable that as many as possible of the lines should be in these directions : thus a north and south line may form one side of the supposed isometrical square which regulates the drawing, and the cross lines will of course be east and west. But it would greatly lessen the utility of isometrical drawing, if square directions only could be delineated by it ; for lines, and consequently the sections above these lines, may be set off in any direction, as on an ordinary plan, by means of the isometrical protractor. Fig. 1, Plate XIX., represents an adit or level of the following bearings and lengths :—

From A to B, — N. 15 W. 2·80 chains.

B to C, — N. 60 E. 6·00 do.

C to D, — N. 25 E. 5·50 do.

The mode of protracting these is minutely described in page 104, and as it simply consists in using the isometrical protractor for setting off the angles in the same manner as by the common protractor, it is evident that the lines of any survey may be thus projected, observing that *the length of all lines not parallel to the isometrical lines* must be found by the method described in page 104, and represented in the diagram, Fig. 1, Plate XIII. Whatever intermediate distances are to be set off on these in-isometrical lines may be first marked on an isometrical line, drawn so as to form an angle with one end of the in-isometrical line, and transferred in the manner described in page 142, and exhibited in Fig. 2, Plate XVII.

The distortion of length in all lines except those which are isometrical, is an inevitable result of those limits which are placed by the laws of vision to the representation of solid objects on a plane surface ; and this difficulty, which constantly exists in the admirable picture delineated on the retina of the eye, cannot by any possibility be overcome by any method of drawing whatever. It is, however, to be observed, that *a similar distortion takes place in every line of a common ground plan or section which departs from the parallelism of the plane on which the drawing is made,* and consequently merely exists in isometrical drawing in common with every other mode of representing objects. In order to exhibit this distortion of length, as it exists in a common vertical section as compared with an isometrical section of the adit A B C D, Fig. 1, Plate XIX., the true length, viz. 14·30, is represented by the line *x,* and the letters *a b c d* indicate the respective places of the points A B C D in the figure above. The line *y* exhibits on a straight line the lengths from A to B, B to C, and C to D, as they appear when drawn isometrically, for as they deviate from what are called the isometrical directions, the apparent length is consequently distorted, and this to the student may appear a considerable imperfection. The proper way, however, to meet this objection, is to enquire by what mode of projection can the sectional workings of a mine be so represented as to exhibit the true length of lines on different planes. If the common modes of parallel projection are used, the distortion of length will often equal, or even exceed, that which occurs in isometrical drawing; thus in the present example, the true length of the whole adit from A to D is 14·30 chains. Isometrical drawing gives the apparent lengths as follow :—

From A to B — 2·425 instead of 2·80
B to C — 7·182 instead of 6·00
C to D — 6·468 instead of 5·50

16·075 instead of 14·30

An orthographic section of the same adit made parallel to the line B C, would present the following results :—

From A to B — ·725 instead of 2·80
B to C — 6·000 being 6·00
C to D — 4·505 instead of 5·50

11·230 instead of 14·30

L

We find, therefore, that the apparent error of the isometrical drawing is 1·775, while that of orthographic projection is 3·07. And, since this imperfection is common to every kind of orthographic projection, it is obvious that isometrical drawing possesses a decided advantage over the usual methods of projection in representing the angles of the object, and in the easy and convenient manner by which the true dimensions can be obtained from the isometrical delineation. In sections of roads and railways, or of any objects comprised in one plane surface, the expedient described in page 153 is resorted to, and the several lengths truly shown without regard to any principles of projection, the same as if the road or railway was in a perfectly straight line; but, for the reasons given in the same page, this process is inapplicable to those interior workings of mines which are situated in different planes; and though nearly all sectional drawings are more or less attended with imperfection, yet, as a scientific method of delineating subterranean workings, isometrical drawing possesses advantages superior to all other methods, and which render it well entitled to the attention of those who are interested in such subjects.

The lines E B, B F, and F D, Fig. 4, Plate XIX, are the true ground plan of the adit of which an isometrical plan is shown in Fig. 1, and as the eye in Fig. 4 is supposed to be exactly above the adit, the vertical face of the section over it is consequently invisible ; whereas, in the isometrical drawing, Fig. 1, in the same plate, not only is the ground plan of the adit shown by the lines A B, B C, and C D, but the oblique position of the eye affords a view of the several strata above it, the delineation of which is here added as an example of the manner in which vertical sections of strata, and also levellings over the surface, may be represented.

The ground over the adit from A to B, on being levelled, is found to rise 10 yards in the first chain, 30 yards at 2 chains from A, and 60 yards at B, above the level of the adit at A. The surface from B to C rises in 2 chains from B, 10 yards at 4 chains, rising other 10 yards, and at C a further rise of 15 yards, making the summit above C, 95 yards above the commencement at A. At 2 chains from C, along the line CD, the fall is 25 yards, at 4 chains, a further descent of 20 yards, and from thence level to the extremity of the adit at D, making the surface at the last place 50 yards in height above the level of A.

Set off with a common scale of 4 chains to an inch, the distances 1·00 and 2·00 on the isometrical line A *h*, and project them by lines drawn parallel to B*k*, on the adit AB, then above these points on AB sett off the respective heights of 10, 30, and 60 yards, and connect them by lines which will represent the surface (in this instance a precipitous face of rock). The distances 2·00 and 4·00 are in like manner to be set off on the line B*k*, and marked by lines parallel to *k*C on the adit BC, whence by vertical lines the results of the levelling can be accurately laid down, and a similar process is repeated on the line CD.

Now it is to be carefully noted that the line ABCD represents an adit perfectly level, but as there is generally more or less rise in such adits for drainage, or to avoid difficult strata, &c., the line ABCD will be more properly considered as a truly level line exactly coinciding in its horizontal bearings with the adit, therefore supposing the latter to rise 1 in 20 it will appear on the isometrical section, Fig. 1, Plate XIX., as shown by the thick black line over ABCD. Hence the process of delineating geological plans and sections is found to consist in the drawing of a plan on a supposed horizontal plane or base, on which all bearings can be set off by the angles of the isometrical protractor, directly from the field-book of the survey, and when the plan is completed, then all manner of vertical objects may be represented above their several positions on the base.

The horizontal plane which is indispensable for obtaining the vertical dimensions of the drawing, having of course no existence in nature, may be familiarly compared to an immense plane of glass placed in the earth in a truly horizontal position, and having on it squares similar to those which have been suggested for defining this horizontal base on the drawing, and which are represented in Plate XX. Hence it is necessary in constructing any isometrical plan, to assume such a convenient position for this plane as may best suit the objects to be represented. For the plan of a large district, the level of the sea is a very proper and convenient base. In an inland district, the level of any principal river, and in a mine, the principal entrance or the level of the principal workings may be adopted. Of course objects may be represented below as well as above the horizontal plane, but it is necessary to keep in view, that the direction of all the principal lines whether above or below the horizontal plane or base, should be marked by dotted lines and corresponding letters of reference, on the said plane, in order that their bearings and relative vertical positions may at any time be readily ascertained.*

* An instrument of frame work for ascertaining heights, &c. on a plan or model, is described in a scarce and curious volume in the possession of the Author, called "the True

The isometrical section, Fig. 4, Plate XVIII, is a supposed portion of an inland district, having a river flowing through it at an elevation of 50 yards above the horizontal plane or base on which the drawing is projected. The dotted line represents the course of the river on the isometrical base, and the double line over it represents the river at an elevation of fifty yards above the plane on which it is projected, and it is obvious that the fall of the river, whether in an even descent, or by cataracts, may be faithfully delineated, as well as the contour and geological structure of the whole of the adjoining country.

The method of transferring plans from one scale to another by means of squares is well known, and copies of horizontal or ground plans may be at once reduced to the isometrical form by simply measuring the points of intersection on the true squares of the orthographic plan, and setting them off on corresponding isometrical

Interest of Great Britain, &c., by Sir Alexander Murray, of Stanhope. In this instrument, and especially in the drawings of it, a near approach is made to isometrical projection, but without discovering those principles which would have enabled the enthusiastic writer to explain his various plans of improvement in a much more clear and scientific manner than is done by the very singular maps and plans contained in the work.

squares.   In this manner the isometrical drawing
of Silver Band mine, Plate XX., is transferred
from the ground plan of the same in Plate III.,
and instead of one general section, as in Plate
III., the isometrical drawing contains a section of
the strata on every vertical plane along the course
of the adits.   The horizontal plane or base on
which this drawing is projected, coincides with
the entrance of the adit or level mouth, and the
strata below the level are shown together with
those which lie between the level and the surface.
The bottom of the adit or level, coinciding with
the horizontal plane, is distinguished by a strong
dotted line, for it is this connection with the
horizontal plane that constitutes the value of this
mode of drawing.

In a first attempt to delineate mine workings in
isometrical drawing, there appears some difficulty
in making a proper distinction between horizontal,
inclined, and vertical lines, for these on an isometrical plan may all be represented by lines parallel
to each other, and yet represent these several
directions.   This inconvenience exists, more or
less, in all drawings, and even in the natural
appearance of objects; as for instance, a post by
a road side, viewed in the direction of the road
appears parallel with it, though the one is upright
and the other flat.   In order to obviate any want

of clearness that may arise from this circumstance,
it is proper to make a distinction between the
different kinds of lines in isometrical drawing, as
follows :

Isometrical lines, including, of course, all vertical lines by continued straight lines.   In-isometrical lines by long thin strokes as in the engraved
reference on Plate XX.   Out-isometrical lines
by short dots.

Lines projected on the horizontal base, by
dots alternately long and short.   Lines connect-
ing the horizontal plan with the isometrical representation above, by very faint and small round
dots.   In many plans a still clearer distinction
may be effected by the aid of colours.

By rigidly adhering to this distinction of the
several different directions represented, the principal inconvenience of isometrical projection is
greatly obviated, viz., the perplexity which arises
from the enlargement or contraction of those lines
which are not in the isometrical directions.   By
the method here suggested, all *continued straight
lines* on an isometrical plan may be measured by
the common scale to which the plan is drawn, as
also may the *small round dotted lines* of connection from the horizontal base to the adits or
other objects above or below, for these small
dotted lines being always vertical, are consequently

isometrical lines. The length of in-isometrical lines may be readily obtained by means either of the isometrical protractor or projecting rulers. The delineation of Fig. 1, Plate XIII., as described in page 104, explains the use of the former instrument, and the rulers may be thus applied either for projecting in-isometrical lines, or for ascertaining their length when drawn.

1st. To set off any given length and bearing from a meridian line by the isometrical rulers, as for example, an adit 5·50 chains long, and bearing N. 25° E.

On the isometrical line which represents the meridian, as at C n″, Fig. 1, Plate XIII., set off the length 4·98, which is the latitude, and apply the isometrical ruler, No. 2, with the edge D E coinciding with the line C n″, and the point E of the ruler coinciding with the north extremity of the distance 4·98. From this extremity draw a line along the edge E A, and upon it set off the distance 2·32, which is the departure. The east extremity of this line will give the true isometrical position of the point D, in the line C D, which is the isometrical delineation of a line 5·50 long and bearing N. 25° E.

To ascertain the length and bearing of the line C D on an isometrical plan, draw an isometrical line C n″ through the point C, apply the ruler

No. 2, as before, the edge D E being on the isometrical line C $n''$, and the edge E A coinciding
with the point D, measure the distance from C
to the point E on the ruler, and also from the
point E on the ruler to the point D, on the
line C D, set off these distances on two lines
forming a right angle, connect the extremities,
and the hypothenuse thus formed is the true
length, and the angle corresponding to $n''$ C D,
is the true bearing of the line C D.

The following example is added as a further
illustration of the application of the projecting
rulers for isometrical drawing.

In Plate XIV., Fig. 5 represents a square,
*a b c d*, on a horizontal plane, on which is delineated an adit 3 $f$ 1. It is required to make an
isometrical representation of the same.

Construct the isometrical square *a' b' c' d'*,
Fig. 6, and set off *c'* 1' equal to *c* 1 in Fig. 5;
and also *a'* 3' equal to *a* 3 in Fig. 1. Apply the
edge A B of ruler No. 1 to the side *c d*, Fig. 5,
until the side of the ruler B C intersects the angle
*f* : measure the distance *c* 2, and 2 *f*, and with the
projecting ruler, No. 3, set off the same distances
in the isometrical directions, viz., *c'* 2' and 2' *f'*,
then draw 1' *f'* and *f'* 3', which gives the isometrical delineation of the adit 3 *f* 1. Geometrical
construction will generally be found the simplest

mode of obtaining the above and similar data for isometrical lines, and by using well-divided scales the results may be obtained with sufficient practical exactness.

For geological and mining plans the isometrical protractor and geometrical construction will be found the most convenient and useful means of setting off in-isometrical lines; but in plans of buildings and machinery, it may be desirable to obtain in-isometrical lengths and bearings from the sector, the use of which, for this purpose, will be explained in the chapter relating to these subjects.

On considering that the occurrence of different kinds of lines on a plane must necessarily require not only a greater degree of care in projecting such lines, but likewise a more abstract consideration in viewing them when drawn, isometrical plans may appear to be attended with a degree of complexity, with which common ground plans and vertical sections are not encumbered. This arises from the circumstance that, in isometrical drawing, *horizontal and vertical lines can be represented in every direction*, while in a common horizontal plan *no vertical lines can be represented at all, neither can any horizontal bearings be shown* on a vertical section.

It has already been observed, how desirable it is to limit the drawing of plans chiefly, and in

most cases entirely, to those objects only, which
have been carefully measured, or concerning the
position of which, no reasonable doubt can exist.
Such plans and sections will appear scanty and
mean as professional works, and by many be
deemed inferior in merit to a rich display of suppositious strata or other objects, coloured so as to
form a handsome picture; but when the relative
size of man, and the means of human observation
are taken into account, it is not surprising that his
knowledge of the vast fabric of the earth, should
be so insignificant in comparison with its stupendous extent.   True sections, unadorned with pictorial groups of strata, and strictly limited to
actual observations, may be less flattering to our
vanity, as well as less pleasing to the eye, than
highly finished and pictorial plans, but a correct
taste, founded on a scientific study of geometrical
drawing, will reject, as much as possible, such
additions, as being not only useless, but also
very frequently deceptive.*   Within this limit of

* This observation must be considered as referring to an
advanced state of geological information, and also as chiefly
relating to plans intended for practical purposes of utility.
At the present time, so few authentic data exist, that it is
frequently necessary, in forming geological drawings, to make
many supposititious additions, and these to a certain extent
will always be more or less required, in general illustrations
of the geology of an extensive district.

actual admeasurement and observation, isometrical drawings will rarely become complicated. On the contrary, the levellings taken over the roads or other parts of an estate, the depth of shafts and strata intersected in them, and the direction, and rise or fall, of the principal underground workings may be combined in isometrical drawings with great clearness and beauty, and thus form such a comprehensive memorial of the works and discoveries made from time to time, as will enable any persons conversant with such plans to ascertain the relative positions of the different parts of the estate, either as regards the minerals or surface objects.

It has been suggested, in a previous chapter, that the working plans of collieries and lead mines should be preserved in regular series, bound together in volumes, and drawn upon squares either engraved or very carefully protracted. For general practical purposes, such a method of preserving ground plans and sections would be superior to any other, inasmuch as the simplicity arising from plans and sections being entirely on one plane must ever render them the ordinary means of recording extensive and complicated workings. The necessity which exists in isometrical drawing, of referring every object to an isometrical plane, renders its application to *all the minute details of*

*extensive subterranean workings* not only tedious
and difficult, but also less explanatory than the
ground plans and sections in common use.
Having, therefore, described the method of constructing isometrical plans, it would greatly mislead
the reader, and especially those who may be disposed to practice isometrical drawing in connection with geology and mining, not to point out
as clearly and distinctly as possible the distinction
between the apparent theoretical advantages, and
the practical utility of this mode of drawing, which
will be best explained by considering to what
extent, and for what purposes, it may be applied
in geological and mining plans.

Isometrical drawings for the illustration of geology and mining may be considered as being
comprised in four classes, viz. to exhibit

    I. THE GEOLOGY OF THE WHOLE, OR ANY CON-
        SIDERABLE PORTION OF A KINGDOM.

    II. THE GEOLOGY OF INTERESTING PORTIONS
        OF DISTRICTS REMARKABLE FOR GEOLOGICAL
        STRUCTURE, OR FOR MINING OPERATIONS.

    III. PLANS AND SECTIONS OF STRATA DISCO-
        VERED IN MINES.

    IV. DRAWINGS OF REMARKABLE GEOLOGICAL
        OBJECTS, AS DETACHED ROCKS, FOSSIL RE-
        MAINS, ETC.

As an example of the 1st class, we may consider

an extent of 500 miles square, a plan of which,
on a scale of 25 miles per inch, would be included
in a square of 20 inches, and an isometrical drawing
of the same would require an area of 22 inches
by nearly 35 inches. Suppose England to be the
country represented, the map must be transferred
to the isometrical drawing by means of squares,
the right hand isometrical lines being used for the
meridian, and the left hand lines consequently
representing east and west lines. The squares
being drawn at distances of 10 or 20 miles, are to
be conceived as representing a plane surface,
coinciding with the level of the sea, upon which isometrical squares the shores are to be drawn with
strong dark lines, but the principal rivers, county
boundaries, and towns, must be faintly traced with
blue colour, or fine dotted lines, on the horizontal
base. The manner of projecting the sections,
whether from drawings previously made, or from
other data, has been already described, and the
nearer the direction of the sections approximates to
the isometrical lines, or north and south, and east
and west directions, so much the more clear and
distinct will be the isometrical representation. A
series of geological sections of England united in
one drawing, in the manner shown in Fig. 4, Plate
XVIII., would not only exhibit the situation of
the strata on and near the surface, but would

also exhibit, by means of the base lines of each section, the sea level carried through from one side of the kingdom to the other, from which, as an index, the height of any part of the sections could be readily ascertained.

In representing so great an extent as 4 or 500 miles, a considerable enlargement of the vertical scale is absolutely necessary. This in the isometrical drawing may be accomplished the same as in ordinary sections, and will be regulated by the distance of the sections from each other. Thus, parallel series of isometrical sections drawn at 5 miles distant will admit of the vertical scale being enlarged 6 or 8 times. If at 10 miles, the enlargement may be 14 times; and if 20 miles is the extent adopted, the vertical scale may be 25 or even 30 times larger than the corresponding scale. The limits of this volume preclude the advantage of giving illustrations on a scale sufficiently large to exhibit the clearness and distinctness with which geological structure might be exhibited in this manner. When the eye becomes accustomed to view isometrical squares, it acquires a power of correcting that distorted appearance which the isometrical angles of 60° and 120° present instead of right angles, and the square lines on the horizontal base afford a ready means of reference for ascertaining the exact geographical position of any portion of the map. Such a representation of the geology of the kingdom would probably be much more popular than ordinary geological maps and sections, and the simplicity of the principles on which such drawings are constructed, by combining an easy method of drawing with an interesting science, would certainly render them a valuable addition to our present means of cultivating a knowledge of geology.

The chief defect in ordinary geological maps is the difficulty of representing a proper line of demarcation between the several formations which frequently overlay each other so near the surface, and so much varied by the natural undulation of the country, that it is almost impossible to define where one should be represented as terminating and the other as commencing. The common vertical sections usually annexed to geological maps certainly afford an explanation, but their detached form renders the position of their respective parts less intelligible than if combined with the plan as in isometrical drawings, the general appearance of which may be rendered more or less attractive according to the care bestowed in finishing it as a landscape drawing.

M

ISOMETRICAL DRAWINGS
OF INTERESTING PORTIONS OF DISTRICTS,
REMARKABLE FOR GEOLOGICAL STRUCTURE,
OR FOR MINING OPERATIONS.

In particular districts, certain geological phenomena are so interesting, or mining operations
so important, as to render plans and sections of
great utility. Notwithstanding, however, the
self-evident truth of this observation, such records have been greatly neglected, even in districts where both the causes above mentioned
combine to render them valuable and important.
The numerous and interesting data concerning
the geology of the coal fields of Northumberland
and Durham, collected by N. J. Winch, Esq.,
and the valuable sections contributed by Messrs.
Buddle, Wood, and others, to the Natural History
Society of Newcastle, evince a laudable desire to
promote a department of science so intimately
blended with some of the chief interests both of
geology and mining. To the class of plans
and sections which are best adapted for the illustration of a particular district, isometrical drawing
is peculiarly well adapted, not, as has already been
observed, as a substitute for, but as a highly interesting and explanatory addition to the ordinary
plans and sections.

Suppose a portion of a district, included in an

area of 10 square miles, to be the subject of iso-metrical representation. The intersecting lines of the horizontal base may be drawn at distances of two inches, thus forming the whole into 100 square miles, on a sheet of drawing paper 3 feet long and 2 feet wide. This base may be considered either as level with the sea, or with any other elevation which may be convenient as a standard of reference, and the position of the coast, rivers, or other conspicuous objects, are then to be delineated upon it, together with the lines of direction along which it is intended to represent vertical sections, observing that it is desirable, if possible, to have them upon or very nearly in the direction of the right and left hand isometrical lines on the horizontal base. Upon this scale, series of parallel sections may be shown at every mile, having a vertical enlargement of three times, which will be nearly 300 yards per inch, and if the country is not greatly elevated above the level assumed, the vertical scale may be 4 or even 5 times the horizontal scale.

When the area is included in a square of 4 or 5 miles in extent, the scale of 400 yards per inch may be adopted in the isometrical drawing, and though the general formation of a district may be clearly shown by the same vertical scale, it will be requisite, in giving any minor details, to adopt an enlargement of the latter, as twice or thrice the horizontal scale.  It must be kept in view, that the vertical scale should never be enlarged except when it is absolutely necessary to render the plan intelligible, and the enlargement, on the same principle, should never exceed that which is sufficient to explain the subject.  Great attention also must be paid to the projection and drawing of the lines, to the brightness and transparency of the colouring, and to the neatness and distinctness of such explanatory lettering or figures of reference as are necessary.

If isometrical drawings were generally used, it would greatly lessen the difficulty of constructing them, and also add to their accuracy, to have isometrical squares of 2 inches each, printed with blue ink from a copper-plate 36 in. by 24 in. Atlas or Double Elephant drawing paper, thus printed, might be sold at a moderate advance on the present price, and paper of less size and inferior quality might also be sold for smaller drawings, or for rough sketches.  If drawing keeps pace with the rapid progress of general improvement, which is now so much and so zealously promoted, it is certain that in all matters wherever mechanical projection is concerned, isometrical drawing will be found to merit a considerable share of attention ; and if geology is studied as it ought to be, by the constant accumulation of facts, isometrical sections of districts will probably be more generally used and better understood than the usual horizontal plans and vertical sections now are.

### ISOMETRICAL DRAWINGS OF THE INTERIOR OF MINES.

The preceding classes of isometrical drawings, comprising the illustration of the geology of a kingdom, or of considerable districts, come within the scope of the study of geology as a science, and the construction of such drawings must greatly facilitate a general as well as local knowledge of the principal features of geological structure. The representation of those further details which are found in prosecuting mining operations may be considered as forming a third class of geological drawings, which, in a regular and scientific system of preserving subterranean records, would form an invaluable arcana of information, condensed in a small compass, and combining great practical utility with the highest importance as materials for the promotion of geological science.

If the several working plans of mines were regularly preserved in volumes of a moderate size, as suggested in Chapter I., it would be desirable to annex to each volume an isometrical representation of the several strata known to exist, which might be called the Geological Plan of the Mine. The objects represented, and the information written on this plan, should relate to the condition of the surface, strata, seams of coal, or veins of lead, as they exist, independently of mining operations; and however difficult it may now be to construct such plans, owing to the long-continued neglect of collecting and preserving the requisite data, it might, in the course of a few years, be rendered an easy and simple task. This will appear very evident to any one who attempts the construction of a geological representation of a mine, with a strict regard to scientific truth. It may be easy to assume supposititious lines of strata, and to fill a drawing with coloured strata throughout a large extent of section; but if, at a subsequent period, shafts or other workings penetrate the plans thus drawn, it is probable that the greatest discrepancies will be found to exist. Hence the necessity, already so often alluded to, of confining the representation on plans to those objects only of which the true position is perfectly known, and of adhering to the strictest geometrical accuracy in the delineation of these respective objects.

THE GEOLOGICAL DRAWING OF A MINE should be on the same scale as the general ground plan,

and the vertical scale must be the same as the horizontal, whether a scale of 2 or 4 chains per inch is
adopted.   The former of these (being 44 yards
per inch) is sufficiently large for distinguishing
the principal strata, seams of coal, or veins; and
the scale of 4 chains, or 88 yards per inch, is $2\frac{1}{4}$
times larger than the vertical scale adopted by Mr.
Buddle, in his sections of the coal fields near
Newcastle.*   By either of these scales, therefore, the principal geological structure of a mine
may be distinctly shown, and the distance at
which parallel sections may be made will depend
upon the depth to be represented.   Thus, parallel
sections having a vertical extent of 100 fathoms
in depth, may be drawn about 10 chains distant,
as in Fig. 4, Plate XVIII., and, as a general
rule, the distance of the parallel sections may be
a fourth or fifth part longer than the depth to be
represented.

This relates to parallel series of isometrical
sections; but in some instances it may be desirable to represent other directions, and it may
require some management also to avoid a con-
fused mixture of too many lines.   This must
necessarily vary in each particular case, and a facility of surmounting this and other difficulties can

* Vide Transactions of Nat. Hist. Society of Northumberland, Durham, and Newcastle upon Tyne.   Vol. I.

only result from that extensive practice which must be afforded by any general adoption of iso-metrical drawings for the purpose of geological illustration. The geological drawing of a mine should exhibit as much as possible of the entire face of each section, with an accurate delineation of the surface over it, projected from actual levelling; and though parallel series might be shown at the several distances already specified, it is obvious that materials could seldom be abundant enough for so many sections. If the isometrical sec-tions are drawn at a considerable distance from each other, the intervening space may be filled up by a representation of the surface of the country, coloured either so as to represent the natural appearance, or to indicate the basseting or cropping out of the several rocks or strata under it.

### DRAWINGS OF FOSSIL REMAINS, ETC.

This interesting branch of geological study has, from its popular nature, been the subject of more frequent and excellent illustration than any other. Curious masses of rock, fossil remains, &c., can-not in many instances be better explained than by ordinary sketches or perspective views, drawn in such a position as best exhibits what is re-markable in their structure, while the dimensions

may be given in letter-press explanations, or de-
noted by figures on the drawing.    Plate XXI.
is an example of such a sketch drawn in ordinary
perspective, and represents a fine specimen of
the fossil trees which are found in the rocks
near the magnificent mansion of A. J. Cresswell
Baker, Esq., at Cresswell, in Northumberland.
With reference to this class of geological drawings, it may be observed, that they furnish excellent subjects for amateur etchings, a department
of art which ought to be much more generally
known and practised than it now is.    Engravers
would find it their interest to afford every facility
to those who have taste and leisure for such an occupation, by furnishing them with copper, etching
grounds, and occasional instructions or assistance
in the management of the acid in biting in, as it is
technically called.    The example in Plate XXI.
is one of the author's first attempts in etching,
and the ease and pleasantness of the process are
such, as he is convinced will form an agreeable
source of amusement to those who possess an
inclination for such pursuits.    For drawings of
this class there is an ease and freedom in common perspective which cannot always be attained
by the more formal rules of projection, which,
therefore, should only be adopted when it affords
some peculiar advantage.    This will be the case

when the object approaches to a cubical form, or
when it is desirable to exhibit the connection of
two or three planes to a uniform scale on one
drawing.

When the several dimensions of such objects
are required with great accuracy, they may be
taken from the originals by means of a vertical
measuring rod placed at certain fixed positions,
and the heights, as well as the lateral distances,
may be measured by a sliding lateral scale, as
shown in Plate XXI.    The several heights may
be then set off by any scale on an isometrical
drawing, and the several lateral distances from the
rod to the object also set off by the same scale
on isometrical lines, and by the enlarged or reduced scale if in-isometrical directions are used.
The points thus correctly laid down may be distinguished by a dotted line, or faint-coloured line,
and the remainder of the example finished by an
eye sketch.

As the drawing of fossil remains and similar
curiosities is peculiarly adapted for the amusement of those who unite science with entertainment, and as the method here briefly described
is also applicable to a great variety of objects, as
antique vases, Roman altars, and in short to all
opaque objects of convenient dimensions, an example is introduced in order to render the details

of the operation perfectly clear and intelligible.

Suppose, for instance, that it is required to make an accurate representation of the fossil tree in Plate XXI., which shall exhibit the various contour of the same at different heights from the ground, and thus afford not merely a general idea, like the etching, Plate XXI., but a medium by which at any time the several dimensions can be ascertained, and if necessary, a model constructed from them.

The line *a a a*, Fig. 2, Plate XXII., is supposed to represent the base of the fossil tree[*] standing on a level floor, on which the square A B C D is correctly measured, each side being two feet in length. The dimensions are to be taken by a rule applied in a direction square across each side, as shown at 1, 2, 3, on the line A C; 4, 5, 6, on the side C D, an the other sides in like manner. These measures may, of course, be taken in any place best suited for delineating the contour of the object, and having obtained the dimensions by the simplest process which can afford the data for making a correct drawing, it becomes extremely easy to transfer the same to paper, and thus the ground plan

* The minute details of form here given are assumed, being drawn from recollection. For an account and principal dimensions of the specimen, see Hodgson's History of Northumberland, Vol. II. Part 2, p. 205.

*a a a* is constructed; and with equal ease, with
the same data, may an isometrical ground plan be
made, as at a a a, Fig. 1, Plate XXII.   From
a perpendicular rod placed at the several points
1, 2, 3, &c., the distance may be measured in the
same directions at any height from the base, suppose 15 inches.   The results of this measurement are represented in Fig. 2, by a strong
dotted line, and the contour at 30 inches from the
base is shown in the same figure by a faint dotted
line.   The vertical lines upon 1, 2, 3, &c., in
Fig. 1, represent the several positions of the rod,
and the direction in which each lateral measurement is made is shown by lines or dots corresponding to those which distinguish the height
measured to.   These form data, by which at any
time the true dimensions may be ascertained, the
places measured to, being marked, remain as
permanent points of reference, and the whole circumference may in this manner be represented, as
in this example is indicated by faint lines.   With
a little dexterity in managing the vertical rod, a
person with the slightest knowledge of drawing
may, by a most simple and easy process, delineate
the most complex forms, and an artist may form,
by lines like those of Fig. 1, Plate XXII., a
correct outline on which to represent the external
features of any object.   In contributions to geological and other public societies, it is obvious

that such a combination of accurate delineation with pictorial effect must be highly interesting, or, as in the present example, the general aspect may form one drawing, and an isometrical outline of dimensions accompany it, as in Plates XXI. and XXII.

It is by an operation similar to what is here described, that the sculptor transfers the dimensions of his original cast or model, to the marble in which the design is to be executed. The clay model and the rough block are each placed on a level base, on the straight edge of which is a scale, with a vertical sliding rod: a lateral rod slides on the vertical one, and is fixed in any position by means of a ball and socket. A similar instrument might often prove of considerable use in establishments, whether of public societies or in manufactories, where accurate mechanical drawings are frequently in request.

It would require large and costly plates to illustrate the various modes in which isometrical drawing might be rendered available in the service of geology. The present work, however, by combining the fullest details of the principles of this mode of drawing, with such examples of its application as are necessary to illustrate the general nature and advantages to be derived from it, will, it is trusted, be found a means of inducing some share of public attention. It is to be kept in view, that no branch of art or science can be suddenly acquired, and the difficulties which at first present themselves must not be considered as final impediments to the cultivation of this useful and interesting method of drawing.   A geological plan of part of Alston Moor, constructed some years ago on the principles of this projection, has met with the unqualified approval of many eminent and experienced scientific and practical men, and on explaining it to the Society of Civil Engineers in London, in May, 1833, I had the honour to receive the thanks of that body.   It is projected on a scale of two chains to an inch, and comprises six separate sections, exhibiting the most interesting portions of the mountain limestone formation.   The aqueduct of Nentforce level, the interior of a leadmine, the disruption caused by the mineral veins, and a large extent of the surface of the country, are all shown in a clear and intelligible manner, on a drawing 28 inches by 22 inches.   Copies of this plan are in the possession of the Institution of Civil Engineers, and of the Natural History Society in Newcastle, its dimensions alone preventing it from being introduced as one of the illustrations of this volume.

From this general outline of the application of isometrical drawing to the illustration of geology, it will evidently appear that the data obtained by mineral surveys may be condensed in a small compass by this method of representing vertical and horizontal planes in one drawing. Let us suppose, for instance, that this principle had been acted upon throughout the great mining fields of this kingdom for the last 50 years, by preserving, on regular series of plans, not only horizontal, but also vertical representations of all the surveys and levellings which have been made in them. A mass of data would have been thus collected in a clear and tangible form; the result of expensive and laborious operations would have afforded the fullest benefit of experience to similar works; the exact position of mineral veins and dykes, and the phenomena caused by them, would have been ascertained in so many places, as to have afforded a clear idea of the probable results in other adjoining districts; and the information contributed by each proprietor would have tended greatly to promote the true interests of all. The levellings made over the surface of a mineral estate, the position and depth of every shaft or boring, with the intersected strata delineated on each, the direction and inclination of the principal subterranean workings, and a record of the several mineral discoveries and operations, would be an invaluable appendage to the deeds of every estate, and every day adds to the necessity for, and value of, such records. The construction of such plans on uniform scales, and with common conventional signs, together with a more general appreciation of the nature of such plans by the public, would in time give fixed and definite means of estimating the value of these subterranean stores of wealth, which are now in a great measure the hidden and mysterious objects of vague and uncertain speculation.    Such an improvement in mineral plans and surveys is assuredly deserving of the attention of not only every land and mine owner, but of every one who is desirous of promoting the permanent interests of the kingdom, which are so interwoven with its mineral products.    The testimony of the highest practical and scientific authorities has been again and again offered with a view to such improvement, and a general outline of operations as regards ordinary plans and sections is given in the first chapter of this work.    To the value, clearness, and popular nature of such mineral records, a great addition may assuredly be made by the appropriate use of those isometrical drawings, which it is the object of this work to introduce to the notice of the public, and which, by combining pictorial effect with geometrical accuracy, and scientific as well as practical use, may greatly contribute to the improvement of this department of practical science.

## CHAPTER V.

### APPLICATION OF ISOMETRICAL DRAWING TO ORNAMENTAL AND LANDSCAPE GARDENING.

THE art of isometrical drawing may be applied with peculiar effect to the picturesque delineation of surface objects, of which none are more beautiful and interesting than the decorations which refined taste and judicious management can produce in the arrangement of gardens and of extensive parks and pleasure grounds. The usual method of representing these is by means of ordinary ground plans, and by landscape views. The former are for the most part executed without regard to pictorial effect, and even if well drawn and richly coloured, are yet incapable of showing the height of the various objects : as to landscape or perspective views, they have been extensively used, and have formed the delightful occupation of many who possess taste and talents for this department of the fine arts. The plan is

stiff and formal, but has the merit of being a
faithful outline; while the landscape drawing, with
all its rich and glowing tints, and aerial perspective,
affords little or no information as to the relative
size and position of the various features of the
scene.    Supposing the plan of a mansion and its
adjacent gardens to be carefully drawn and coloured, as they would appear to an eye placed exactly above them; the roof only of the house being
visible, all traces of the windows, or of any architectural enrichments of its walls, would be totally
hidden; while, also, a small cottage and a lofty
steeple could only be represented by the outlines
of the space they occupy on the ground.    In
landscape sketches or paintings, a bush in the
foreground exceeds in magnitude the majestic oak
in the distance, and the representation is limited
to the apparent size and position of objects, as
seen from one point of view.

Artists who have had occasion to delineate
views of this description, have attempted various modes of combining the separate advantages of the plan and perspective view, in order to
unite accuracy with beauty; and it is amusing in
various old books, to observe the singular efforts
made to produce this desirable union.    Sometimes the house is drawn as though it lay prostrate
on the earth; and this mode of forcing an elevation

on a ground plan occurs in many county maps, and in plans of Towns and Estates. Sometimes a bird's-eye view is adopted, and the whole scene thrown into formal perspective, thus sacrificing the graceful ease and freedom of a picture, without gaining the advantages of a plan.

Mr. Loudon, in his excellent Encyclopædia of Agriculture, and in others of his valuable publications, offers some interesting suggestions relative to such delineations, and justly comments on the improving taste, which requires a corresponding improvement in this department of drawing. Isometrical drawing forms a medium between the two kinds of representation now generally used. In its principles, as well as in the manner of its application, it possesses the intrinsic geometrical qualities of a ground plan, and at the same time admits of the pictorial delineation of vertical objects ; hence all the various compartments of a garden may be protracted by a scale, and the various trees and plants represented by the same scale, together with the mansion, terraces, or other features of the scenery. The construction of isometrical drawings of ornamental grounds is unattended with the numerous and complicated projection of lines which are indispensable in ordinary perspective, and is so easy of attainment that any one, by considering the practical illustrations already given, may easily produce the representation of any surface objects.

It has been shown in what manner a rectangular object may be represented, either by means of compasses or the projecting rulers. When a garden or pleasure ground, therefore, approximates to this form, the surface lines can be easily projected by the same methods which are used in delineating the various objects on the upper surface of the cube in Plate I X. (see page 130); the seveveral compartments into which that surface is divided may be considered as representing variously-shaped portions of garden ground, on which trees and shrubs, with the walks and ornamental borders, &c., may be delineated by a uniform scale. When once the principle is clearly understood, there can be no difficulty in applying it on an extensive scale, and thus, with the requisite measurements, or with plans to copy from, an isometrical representation of houses and pleasure grounds may be easily and pleasantly drawn. The same remark applies to extensive woodlands, where the undulation of the ground forms a conspicuous feature ; and, still more, if abrupt precipices, or steep and sudden eminences, add romantic interest to the scene. Of such grounds, the common horizontal plan affords a very inadequate idea, while the isometrical projection enables the artist to delineate the exact surface lines in any required direction.

When either the boundaries or any other portions of the grounds are in irregular directions, their position can be readily obtained by a similar process, on a larger scale to that by which the outline of the base of the Fossil Tree, in Plate XXII., is represented.

In that plate, the irregular figure *a a a*, in Fig. 2, may be conceived to be the boundary line of a field, or garden, as it would appear on an ordinary plan, the measurement of which, and subsequent isometrical delineation, depend on the simple process of surrounding it by rectangular lines, and taking offsets to the several points. In like manner, any interior walks or divisions may be obtained by continuing lines across from opposite sides of the rectangle, and measuring the points of intersection, or the length of offsets to the requisite places intended to be delineated. The rectangular lines thus made use of, as at AC and CD, in Fig. 1., Plate XXII., are the right and left hand isometrical lines on which, or on any lines parallel with them, the dimensions of the ground can be ascertained by a process, which though extremely simple, is certainly less so than what is required in ordinary ground plans. When, however, the

N 3

isometrical plan of a garden or pleasure ground is obtained, it possesses this great superiority over the common ground plan, that elevations of any kind can also be projected on it, and hence the various terraces, trees, houses, or other objects, can be represented with great pictorial force and beauty.

In Plate XXIII., Fig. 1 represents the ground plan of a garden; and Fig. 2 exhibits the isometrical representation of the same, and though necessarily drawn on a very limited scale, the effect of this projection is rendered sufficiently obvious to show how much it is applicable to drawings of this description.

*Every vertical* and *all the principal horizontal lines* can thus be delineated by a common scale on one drawing, and afford the means of accurately representing every variety of surface by an exact and extremely simple process. It appears to me that the difference between a strict isometrical *projection*, and that more convenient enlargement which admits of the same scale as the common ground plan, and which I distinguish by the term isometrical *drawing*, has not been sufficiently attended to. The great advantage gained by this enlargement or drawing, as distinguished from strict projection, was particularly detailed in the observations which I submitted to the Society of

Civil Engineers, and is explained in Chapter III. of the present work. Most of the examples, however, which have been given to the public, are *projections* of the respective objects represented, so that to delineate them it is necessary to find the proportion between the true scale and the reduced isometrical scale.

To the gardener, as well as to the geologist or miner, who should attempt to make plans or drawings, this reduction to an isometrical scale causes much additional trouble, without answering any useful purpose; whereas in the isometrical plans and drawings of this work no such perplexity occurs; the same scale which measures the ground plan or elevation, measures also the corresponding parts of the isometrical drawing, the great facility and advantages of which, in preference to true projection, cannot be too strongly impressed on the attention of all who desire to apply this method of drawing to useful purposes.

In geological and mining plans, the isometrical plan or drawing is the only method by which horizontal and vertical objects can be conveniently represented on one plane surface; but in the delineation of gardens and pleasure-grounds the methods described in page 144 may be frequently used, and will be found greatly to facilitate the draughtsman in exhibiting the surface of gardens

or pleasure grounds from actual measurement.
Fig. 1, Plate XXIV, is a *verti-lateral plan* of the
garden represented in the preceding plate, and so
far as lineal dimensions are concerned it may be
considered a species of isometrical delineation.
This method of drawing exhibits, as its name is
intended to express, *a vertical elevation*, and a
*lateral or side view*, combined with the plan; and
when the dimensions are known, the construction,
as has already been explained, is extremely simple,
especially if the isometrical rulers are used, as
shown in Plate XVII, and described in page 145.
Fig. 2, Plate XXIV, is a *verti-horizontal plan*
of the same garden.  With a *vertical elevation*, it
shows a view of the surface very nearly approaching to a *horizontal* or ground plan; and on inspecting both these figures, the principal lines of
direction will be found to correspond exactly with
those in Fig. 1, Plate XXIII, while at the same
time they present a graphic and pictorial effect,
much more interesting than the plans in ordinary
use.  In illustrations of works on architecture
and gardening, so easy and ready a method
of combining architectural elevations with the
plans of adjoining grounds will often be found
extremely interesting and useful; and the use of
the triangular or isometrical rulers reduces the
operation to the utmost possible simplicity; so

much so, that any one who can understand the first principles of ordinary planning and drawing may very soon acquire a correct knowledge of, and practical dexterity in, these several methods of isometrical drawing.

Ornamental and landscape gardening is a pursuit which more than any other requires the union of the plan and picture in one drawing; and the engraved illustrations in works on this subject are often greatly wanting in clearness, from not possessing the desirable union of dimensions and landscape effect, which isometrical drawing produces. The attentive consideration of the principles laid down in the preceding portions of this work, and a little practice in the use of the projecting rulers will soon enable any one to delineate the various surface forms of gardens and pleasure grounds, and to represent upon them the several vertical objects which are situated on them. Fig. 2, in Plate XIX., is a ground plan of an ornamented pleasure ground, in which the elevations of the rising ground are shown, and the reference by similar letters to Fig. 3 will convey a correct idea of the manner in which the undulation of surface is represented, the process being exactly similar to that used in the construction of the geological sections in Plate XVIII., the addition of surface-shading,

with trees, &c. being effected by ordinary landscape drawing. For the old English style of
gardening, with its formal hedgerows, and stately
terraces and ballustrades adjoining the mansion,
isometrical drawing is well adapted, and hence,
as one of the illustrations of this subject, I have
availed myself of the permission of Sir John
Swinburne to copy an old painting of Capheaton, while it partook of this character, an
isometrical delineation of which forms the frontispiece of the present work.* Where improve-

* Leland describes this mansion as " A Faire Castle in the
midste of Northumberland as in the bredthe of it, and is the
oldist house of the Swinburnes." Collins, in his Baronet-
age, iii., 174, says, "It was moated about, and had a draw-
bridge, and was a place of resort in the moss-trooping times,
when the gentlemen of the country met together to oppose
those felonious aggressors upon the goods and chattels of
the country, having a beacon on its top to alarm the neighbourhood." It was re-built in 1668, upon a new site a little
to the east of it, from designs by Robert Trollop, the architect of the old Exchange, in Newcastle. Sir William, the
son and successor of the builder, in a letter to Collins, says
that his father demolished the old castle, and rebuilt, in the
same place, a goodly house after the modern fashion, with
courts, garden, and bowling green. These, and numerous
other details respecting the family history and mansion of
the Swinburnes, are given by Hodgson, in his History of
Northumberland. He adds, that " a large bird's eye view of
this building is still preserved here, just as it was left by

ments on an extensive scale are meditated in the
landscape scenery of a district, correct isometrical
drawings are well adapted to exhibit the present
aspect and proposed appearance; and in the hands
of a skilful artist will be found most useful and
highly explanatory additions to the present methods of surface delineations.

Isometrical drawing, from the great ease and

Trollop, with the family of the builder issuing from the
gates to meet a party of their neighbours, the Loraines of
Kirkharle, come on a visit, and the family coach (one of the
very few at that time kept in the county) is introduced in
full equipage, to give effect to the courteous ceremony."
The present baronet, Sir John Swinburne, has made great
improvements and alterations in the body of the house, from
designs by Newton ; but the bold projecting cornice and
richly-carved cantilivers of Trollop's Italian roof, have been
replaced by mouldings and dentils less in unison with the
unique and striking assemblage of rustic pilasters, carved
window jambs, dials, and flower pots of the former design,
which still remain. The ornamented door-way and heraldic
tablet are removed from the centre of the front to the east
end, and the carved pillars of the gateway now adorn the
entrance of an approach which leads to the house through
a deep and extensive grove of old forest trees.

To this brief notice of Capheaton, I cannot but add how
much I feel indebted to its worthy and much-esteemed
owner, for access to several old plans and drawings of the
house, and for many marks of encouraging friendship and
patronage, in the course of my professional occupations.

simplicity of its first principles, and from the convenient and rapid manner of executing it by means of projecting rulers, together with the explanatory and interesting nature of the drawings when completed, is extremely well adapted for the occasional amusement of those who have taste and leisure to cultivate such pursuits.    Such ladies as are tolerably skilled in landscape and flower painting, may find a new and agreeable range of occupation by combining these accomplishments with isometrical delineation.    By measuring a garden or pleasure ground in two directions at right angles with each other, and transferring the dimensions thus gained to isometrical squares, the horizontal shape or ground plan is easily obtained, and the several vertical objects being added in their respective positions, a general outline of the whole is thus formed, which may be enriched with the various colours and ornamental details of the objects represented. In like manner, by using the simple apparatus of an upright measuring rod, with a moveable cross scale, any objects, such as antique vases, altars, &c. may be measured and drawn isometrically, as has already been described in the instance of the fossil tree ; and this easy and mechanical, yet perfectly correct, mode of drawing such objects also opens out a new and entertaining source of occupation to those who have inclination and leisure to follow it. The interest of such pursuits is not confined to the immediate object of such drawings, but extends to a still wider and more useful range of intellectual improvement. Geometry and mathematics are eminently calculated to strengthen and improve the understanding, and in female education in this country they seldom obtain that consideration which they so eminently deserve. Much might be said in support of this observation ; but it would be foreign to the object of the present work to advert to it otherwise than in brief terms. The elaborate study of these sciences is what few ladies can have any reasonable motive for prosecuting, but a general idea of the first great principles by which knowledge can be most truly acquired, ought certainly to obtain some share of diligent attention ; and the first book of Euclid, impressed on young minds, would assuredly tend, in a very efficient manner, to form a correct habit of thinking, and of resting conviction on proper sources of authority. Geometry also obtains no small share of female attention, almost unconsciously bestowed in the formation of many ingenious and ornamental works, but which has reference to no higher object. While isometrical drawing is, therefore, an easy and pleasant amusement, it also partakes so much of geometrical construction as

naturally to invite the attention to the consideration of its principles; and the study of these will
be found to facilitate the knowledge of perspective
drawings as well as of charts, maps, and plans,
which are every day becoming more extensively
used in general literature. Art and science, of
every kind, claim kindred with the best feelings
that can animate our minds. Astronomy, lifting
the soul in contemplation to heaven. Geology
placing before us the stupendous records of crea-
tion. Botany enriching the varied surface of the
globe with delightful interest; and Mineralogy
opening to our view the hidden glories of a subterranean world. To an acquaintance with these
and other sciences, art furnishes us with captivat-
ing and efficient aids, of which the diligent cultivation is not less the duty and interest of individuals than the foundation of national welfare and
prosperity.

The constant tendency of a cultivated taste, in
any of the various departments of art and science,
is to banish from the mind those frivolous thoughts
and pursuits which infringe so much on the hap-
piness alike of individuals and of society at large.
Considerations of this kind might be much extended, and they are here alluded to, as forming
some recommendatory plea for submitting to the
attention of ladies a method of drawing, which at

first sight may appear unsuited for them, on account of that connection with geometry, which, so
far from being deemed an objection, is here respectfully urged as an additional claim for isometrical drawing being favoured with a share of
their attentive study and occasional practice.

As an example of the manner in which isometrical drawing may be applied to ornamental as
well as useful purposes, I have introduced, on
the title page, a vignette view of Chesterholme,
the residence of my much-esteemed and highly-
valued friend, the Rev. Anthony Hedley. This
beautiful little cottage, or antiquarian villa, as it
may justly be termed, with its adjoining gardens
and terraces, forms a striking example of landscape
and architectural beauty, though situated in a district where the general aspect of the scenery is
wild and forbidding. This vignette presents the
appearance of the cottage as it suddenly bursts
on the view on descending the steep approach on
the northern side of Borcum-hill, nearly midway between Haydon Bridge and Haltwhistle, in
the county of Northumberland.*

* The following description of Chesterholme and its adjacent scenery, is from the Supplement to the Gentleman's
Magazine, August, 1833, and forms a suitable explanation
and accompaniment to the title-page vignette :—

" At the head of the gorge, and immediately below the

The process of drawing this and similar objects
isometrically, depends entirely on the few and

meeting of the Craiglough and the Brooky burns, stands
*Chesterholme,* in a lovely and sequestered spot, " procul arte,
procul formidine novi."    It is a sweet picture of mosaic
work inlaid upon an emerald gem : a cottage in the Abbots-
ford style upon one of those charming green holms or mea-
dows bordering upon a river, which in Northumberland are
very generally called haughs.    The heath-headed and
pillar-crowned mountain of Borcum towers above it on the
south-east.    On the west, a steep green bank has its brow
compassed with the ruins of the ramparts of the Roman
station of Vindolana.    On the north, two woody denes,
branching off at a neat farm-house, wind away in different
directions through rising pasture grounds, which skirt the
borders of the sky; and on the south a mountain stream
glides from pool to pool through broad crevices of dove-
coloured marble, under a rustic wooden bridge, till it is suddenly thrown aside by a high sandstone cliff, dappled with
lichens, and overhung with variegated woods.    All this en-
chanted bowl has sides as chastely ornamented with works
of nature and design, as the shield of Achilles was with
works of art.    It is, indeed, like the bowls which Virgil
speaks of, " Asperum signis," crisply carved with figures.
I do not know where I could take an admirer of simple
scenery and antiquarian objects better than to the cottage
of Chesterholme.    About its sunny garden, fragments of
the pillars of antient baths and temples are entwined
with roses or climbing plants.    The cottage is chiefly built
of stones carved by Roman hands, and one of the doors
opens upon the tree-fringed sides and rocky channel of

simple principles and rules which have been detailed in the preceding portions of this work. It is necessary to consider which two of the sides of any rectangular building it is most desirable to exhibit, and having made the selection, the base lines of these sides form the right and left hand isometrical lines, from which the several parts of the building are to be projected, in the manner described at page 130. If the plan of the building is irregular, its several projections can be easily drawn by means of off-sets from rectangular lines,

Chinely burn, where the hazels, and heg-berry, and alder and broad plane trees, and the undying sounds of waters are seen and heard through a passage formed of altars and bas-reliefs, with a cordon of broad stones pierced with lewis holes, and which once supported the battlements of the walls and gates of Vindolana." An arcade has also been formed here, for the reception of antiquities found in the adjacent station, which contains some exceedingly fine altars lately discovered by the owner, several inscribed stones, and other curiosities. The design was given by John Green, Esq., of Newcastle, and is happily suited to the nature of the residence and the character of the adjacent scenery. The interior is chiefly fitted up with Butternut and Cedar. The former wood, though not much known in this country, is well adapted for doors, shutters, presses, &c. It has a rich figure, is easily worked, and has less tendency to warp or twist than many other woods. In appearance it has a near resemblance to oak, and is considerably less expensive.

o

as shown in Plate XXII.; and the outline of the
house being thus obtained, vertical lines drawn
from the several angles to any given height will
complete the representation of those respective
sides of the building which are towards the direction in which the eye is supposed to be placed.
The windows, doors, or other objects on the walls
can be set off in the manner shown in Fig. 1,
Plate XVII., and a very little practice will soon
enable any one to add the several lines of the
roof, and chimneys, &c., simply by considering
what relation they bear to horizontal and vertical
lines.   The architectural outline being thus completed, the shadows and other pictorial additions
may be added according as taste and fancy may
direct.   The chief advantage which isometrical
drawing affords is in the easy and rapid construction of designs; and it may also be observed, that
by supposing the light to fall in any particular
direction, the proper strength and direction of
the shadows may be determined with much greater
ease and certainty than in ordinary perspective
drawings.

From these examples it will readily appear how
much the art of isometrical drawing is adapted to
various departments of landscape and ornamental
gardening.   In the improvement of land, the
laying out of plantations and pleasure grounds,

the formation of gardens and terraces, or the ornamental representation of such as already exist, isometrical drawing exhibits both the plan and picture at a single glance, and in a more clear and intelligible, as well as more simple and correct, manner, than by any other kind of perspective representation. In the sale of mansions, isometrical views showing the several erections and adjoining grounds, would give a faithful idea of their dimensions and relative positions; and, in short, would be found at once a pleasing study for amateur artists, a useful means of information for a variety of practical purposes, and an intelligible and easily-acquired method of delineation for the illustration of books on subjects connected with landscape and ornamental gardening.

## CHAP. VI.

---

### APPLICATION OF ISOMETRICAL DRAWING TO PLANS OF BUILDINGS AND MACHINERY,

#### AND TO GENERAL PURPOSES OF

### CIVIL ENGINEERING.

---

THOSE who are much accustomed to the construction or inspection of architectural or engineering plans and sections, acquire a facility in combining the information given by the separate drawings; but the general observer is often unable to comprehend the relation of the several parts of a design represented in them. The elevation of the church and house, Fig. 2, Plate IX, would lead many persons to suppose that these buildings are in juxta position; and the elevation of the church, in Fig. 3, affords no general idea of the form of the structure; so that to arrive at a correct idea of the form and relative position of these objects, the several drawings, Figs. 1, 2, and 3, must be examined, and the relation of one to the other ascertained by combining them together in the mind. But when the three several planes, the ground plan, and front and end elevations, are united in one drawing, as in Fig. 4, no one can be at a loss to understand the appearance and position of the respective buildings. The picture thus formed strikes the eye with a force and clearness which leave no room for misapprehension; and when to this pictorial effect is added the recommendation, that every part of such drawing can be projected or measured by the same common scale used in the ordinary plan or elevation, it is obvious that for plans and drawings connected with architecture, mechanics, and engineering, isometrical drawing admits of a much more useful and general application than it has hitherto obtained.

Such isometrical plans and drawings are proposed, not as substitutes for, but as highly-explanatory accompaniments of ordinary plans and sections; and the following remarks are intended to point out more expressly the manner in which they may be used with advantage for ordinary purposes, in these respective departments of art and science.

The first application which I shall here describe is to designs for public works, such as the formation or improvement of harbours, the erection or alteration of public buildings, &c. In such designs, for the reasons alluded to with reference to

o 3

Plate IX., it is often extremely difficult to convey
a correct idea by means of ordinary plans and
sections, either of what has been done, or of what
remains to be accomplished.    To the promoters
and supporters of all extensive undertakings which
admit of graphic illustration, it is most desirable that such illustrations should be rendered as
interesting and intelligible as possible; and isometrical plans and drawings will, in many instances,
give a much clearer idea, than any other method of
delineation.    Thus, in the design for a county
prison, Plate XXVI., the isometrical view exhibits at one glance the principal front and end
elevations, with the relative position of the several
buildings, much more clearly and distinctly than
the detached ground plan and separate elevations
of the same buildings in Plate XXV.*    A well-

---

* This plate is reduced from an original design by the
Author, which was submitted to the Commissioners for erecting a new gaol and house of correction in Newcastle upon
Tyne, in 1822, when, in consequence of a public advertisement, several other plans, by architects in London and
Newcastle, were also offered for their consideration.    The
advertisement required the designs to be as plain as the
nature of the building would admit, and hence the present
design has no pretensions to architectural effect ; but the
Commissioners very properly departed from this intention, by
allowing considerable scope to the taste and talents of
Mr. Dobson, whose plan was adopted.    A model of the

executed and neatly-coloured isometrical drawing of such designs approaches more nearly to the effect of a model than any other possible mode of drawing; and whether for public edifices, or for private residences, isometrical designs, by combining a correct geometrical plan with pictorial effect, become much more popular and more easily understood than ordinary plans and sections. Another wide and important field for the introduction of isometrical drawing is to be found in its adaptation to engraved illustrations of works of art and science; a purpose for which it is so peculiarly suited, that it would be useless to comment on it further than by observing, that the distinction, which in the present work has been so expressly stated, of isometrical *drawing* as distinguished from *projection*, should be constantly kept in view, and the former invariably adopted.

A third and extremely useful application of isometrical drawing is to working plans and drawings, not only of buildings and machinery, but also in various other departments of business, as

design represented in Plate 26 was made at the request of the Commissioners, who presented the Author with ten guineas, at that time a gratifying recompense for the labour bestowed on the first attempt at architectural design he had ever made.

carpentry, the manufacture of cabinet furniture, and other similar employments, where working drawings are required. Its fitness for this purpose is very clearly explained in Professor Farish's paper, already alluded to; and those who are at all conversant with such drawings require only a knowledge of the first principles of isometrical projection to enable them to apply it generally to designs of this nature. For the explanatory plans and drawings to accompany specifications of patents, isometrical delineation is well adapted; and if once generally introduced into practice, many other applications of it will naturally arise.

To point out in detail these various applications would occupy a volume of considerable extent, and require a great number and variety of plates of larger size than those contained in the present volume. Such a work, consisting of coloured plates, with brief letter-press explanations, might be rendered extremely useful and interesting by a judicious selection of geological, landscape, architectural, and mechanical subjects; and such a series of isometrical delineations the author would be glad to undertake, but for other and more important avocations, which fully occupy his time and attention. To any one disposed to throw this further light on the subject of isome-

trical drawing, he would willingly render any information or assistance in his power, with access
to several materials for such a publication now in
his possession.

For the method of drawing isometrical plans
of buildings in any required direction, the reader
is referred to Plate XIV., and its explanation in
pages 108 and 111; and as further examples of
the application of this mode of drawing, the
frontispiece View of Capheaton, the vignette of
Chesterholme, the church and house in Plate
IX., the examples of the plans of interior and
exterior of houses in Plates XVII. and XIX.,
the walls and green-houses in Plates XXIII.
and XXIV., and the prisons in Plate XXVI.,
clearly exhibit the effect that is produced by
adopting this singularly easy and effective mode
of representation. The same principles which
have been explained in reference to these, apply
to every possible description of buildings, subject
of course to those limitations which the laws of
vision impose on all drawings.

In representing towers and other similar structures, it is optional to consider them as being
viewed either from above or below. In Plate
IX. the spectator is supposed to be looking down
upon the tower of the church, and consequently
the roof or covering is visible; but if the same

tower were drawn isometrically from below, then
the corner nearest to the eye would be the highest, and of course conceal the roof.  So, in like
manner, when the interior of a church, or an
apartment of any kind, is drawn isometrically, if
it be the object of the artist to show the walls and
floor, he must adopt the higher point of view,
and suppose the roof or ceiling removed in order
to gain a view of the interior; but if the intention
is to show the walls and interior of the roof or
ceiling, then of course the contrary line of direction is assumed, and the floor is conceived to
be removed to afford a view upwards toward the
ceiling.   On inspecting the isometrical representation of the tower, Fig. 1, Plate XXX., it
cannot but occur to every one how very much
this perspective resembles the actual appearance
of a tower when the observer is near to its base,
a circumstance which adds greatly to the value of
this kind of representation as applicable to buildings, since it adds boldness and picturesque freedom, and a natural aspect, to what might at first
appear a formal and ungraceful perspective.  Some
objects, from their position, present a very striking appearance, when viewed in the direction
which isometrical projection supposes.   The monument of Professor Dugald Stewart, (a structure which offers to the delighted eye one of the

finest and purest examples of Grecian architecture), stands on the verge of a rocky promi-
nence of the Calton Hill, at Edinburgh, and, on
a near approach, presents an excellent illustration
of isometrical drawing. This, with its general
position and effect, are indicated by the small
sketch, Fig. 2, Plate XXX., which is to be considered merely as an index to explain the manner
in which a larger isometrical drawing of this or
similar objects might be constructed. The admirable details of this structure, of St. Nicholas'
steeple in Newcastle, and of various cathedral
and other structures, would be admirable subjects
for such a book of illustrations of isometrical
drawing as I have already alluded to. When an
architectural design of a church or mansion is
made on a large scale, the various decorations,
pews, furniture, or other objects, may be admirably introduced, and, by a skilful distribution of
colours and shadows, a very pleasing and highly
illustrative effect may be produced, which could
not fail in giving a more lively conception to the
parties interested in the same, and possibly prevent many misapprehensions which are apt to
occur with those who do not perfectly understand
the plans, sections, and elevations in common
use.

In machinery, many of the principal lines of

frame-work, &c., are either perpendicular, or in horizontal squares, and therefore such lines can be very easily and accurately represented. Lines of whatever kind, which diverge from isometrical directions, are to be drawn by the methods described in Chapter II., the rules of which embrace every possible direction and position both of right lines and circles. The construction of an isometrical ellipse to represent any required circle or wheel, is given at page 114 and sequel, and the position of the wheel in machinery is easily determined by simply remembering that the minor axis of the ellipse always coincides with the axle of the wheel. The circumference of an isometrical wheel may be divided into any number of parts, equal or unequal, either by means of the isometrical protractor, or by following the method shown in Plate XV., Fig. 2, where, by setting off the required divisions on the line BE, intersecting the requisite divisions on the quadrant inscribed between AB and AE, the same may be at once transferred to the isometrical ellipse inscribed in the isometrical square B C D E. Thus cog and pinion wheels, &c., of every description, may be readily drawn, and, when completed and neatly shaded, the isometrical wheel forms the most explanatory representation of such objects that can be made, showing, in equal proportions, the face and edge of the wheel, with the number, thickness, and projection of the teeth or pinions; see Plate XXX., Fig. 3.

In drawing a wheel isometrically, the first thing necessary is to ascertain the position or direction of the axle. Having done this, find by measurement, or by given dimensions, what part of the centre of the axis coincides with the front face or side of the wheel. Then also mark on the same axis, a point in its centre coinciding with the other face of the wheel. If the axis is an isometrical line, the distance between these two points will be exactly equal to the breadth of the edge of the wheel, as measured by a common scale; but if the axle is an in-isometrical line, the relative position or distance of the two points must be found by the rule which applies to in-isometrical lines, in Chap. II. In this instance, also, the two points will represent and correspond with the apparent breadth of the edge of the wheel, though the distance cannot be measured by a common scale, but must be ascertained by reference to an isometrical line, or by the use of the sector. When the points are determined upon the axis, each must form the centre of an isometrical ellipse representing a circle, and, as has been already observed, the minor axis of each ellipse must coincide with the direction of the axle. The

diameter of the wheel being given, the major axis
of the isometrical ellipse will be longer than the
diameter in the ratio of 1 to ·81649, and the
minor axis of the ellipse, which falls upon the line
of the axle of the wheel, will be shorter than the
diameter in the ratio of ·57401 to ·81649.   For
the method of describing the ellipse see Prop.
XVIII., page 113.   For mechanical drawings, it
would be extremely useful for the artist to construct a large diagram, similar to Fig. 1, Plate
XI., having a number of lines parallel with the
hypothenuse XZ, on which should be set off a
scale of feet and inches on the base XY.   Then
if it be required to represent a wheel of any given
diameter, say 10 feet isometrically, the axle of the
wheel being an isometrical line, measure the distance 10 feet from Y towards X, which distance
may be supposed to be represented at P; then is
the hypothenuse P q, the major axis of the isometrical wheel to be drawn at right angles through
the centre of the axis, and the perpendicular Y q
is the minor axis to be set off on the line of the
axis on each side of the centre of the wheel.
Through the same centre, draw two intersecting
isometrical lines on the face of the wheel, and
set off on them by a scale the true diameter, and
thus 8 points or indices are gained from which
the proper ellipse can be easily constructed.   It

will evidently appear, that if the line of the axle is a right hand isometrical line, then the plane face of the wheel will be in a left hand isometrical plane, and *vice versa*. Also, if the axis be vertical, the face of the wheel will be a horizontal plane. When the main lines and wheels deviate much from isometrical directions, it is proper to observe, that some degree of perplexity will arise to the unpractised student, which can only be mastered by a careful and patient consideration of the principles of this projection: difficult and complicated, however, as such examples may occasionally appear, it is certain that both the principles and practice of construction are incomparably more simple and readily understood than any other kind of perspective representation. A facility in the manner of projecting in-isometrical lines, and of ascertaining their length when drawn, as described in page 169, will be found extremely useful in drawing plans of machinery; and as a further aid, the sector may be found useful in the hands of those accustomed to use it.

As this valuable instrument is comparatively little known and seldom used by many practical men, and as it admits of very useful application in this projection, it may be desirable to add the following description of it.

### DESCRIPTION AND USE OF THE SECTOR IN ISOMETRICAL DRAWING.

The sector is an ingenious and useful mathematical instrument for dividing a right line into any number of equal parts ; for forming a universal scale of equal parts ; for setting off angles of any given radius, &c., provided that the scale or radius be within the compass of the instrument; they are constructed of ivory and brass, and one of them is included in every complete case of drawing instruments. The sector consists of two equal legs connected by a folding joint, round which the legs may be opened and shut at pleasure, and the best instruments are constructed with a French joint, which admits of smaller distances being measured than can be done with the common jointed sectors.

In order to effect the purposes for which the sector is designed, straight lines are drawn upon the flat faces from the centre of the joint to the other extremity, and these lines are graduated into scales of equal parts, scales of chords, scales of sines, scales of tangents, &c. These lines are called sectorial lines, and are distinguished by initial letters C for chords, S for sines, T for tangents, and L for lines. The graduations are numbered from the centre, which is therefore called zero, or nothing.

The sectorial lines of each kind are double, one being on each leg of the instrument, and the corresponding lengths or distances from the centre are all equal.

As the chord of 60°, the sine of 90°, or the tangent of 45°, is equal to the radius, the two lines of chords end in 60°, the two lines of sines in 90°, and the two lines of tangents in 45°. The distance between the points 60° and 60° on the line of chords is equal to the distance between the points 90° and 90° of the line of sines, and also equal to the distance between the points 45° and 45° of the line of tangents, at any angle which the legs may form when opened.

Hence an angle cannot be made at one operation by the line of chords more than 60°, nor by the line of tangents more than 45°.

In each pair of scales, the divisions are numbered from zero in the centre of the joint to 10, 20, 30, &c., except the line of equal parts, which is numbered 1, 2, 3, &c., to 10.

The distance between the corresponding points in any pair of lines is called the *transverse distance*, and the distance from the centre to each corresponding point is called the *lateral distance*. Hence the two lateral distances form the two equal sides, and the transverse distance the base of an isoselis triangle. The figures 1, 2, 3, &c., on the lines of equal parts, may represent 10, 20, 30, &c., 100, 200, 300, &c., 1000, 2000, 3000, &c.; and according to the value attached to these figures, will be the value of the intermediate parts. Denominations smaller than the intermediate divisions must be determined by the accuracy of the eye.

### TO SET THE SECTOR TO ANY GIVEN RADIUS.

Enlarge or diminish the angle of the sector, as the case may require, until the transverse distance between the brass points at the extremities of the two lines of chords, or of the two lines of sines, or the two lines of tangents, be equal to the given radius, and the sector will be set.

### THE SECTOR BEING SET, TO FIND THE CHORD, SINE, OR TANGENT OF ANY NUMBER OF DEGREES.

Take the transverse distance between the points at the numbers denoting the degrees in the lines which are of the same species as the line required, whether it be a chord, sine, or tangent, and this distance will be the chord, sine, or tangent to the number of degrees required.

### EXAMPLES.

The sector being previously set to any given radius within the scope of the instrument,

### EX. I. TO FIND THE CHORD OF 20°,

Set one of the points of the compass on the point 20, in one of the lines of chords, and extend the other point to 20 in the other line of chords; the distance between these points will be the chord of 20° to the radius between the brass points 60 and 60 of the line of chords.

### EX. II. TO FIND THE SINE OF 25°.

Set one point of the compass on 25 in one of the lines of sines, and extend the other to 25 in the other line of sines, and the distance will be the sine of 25° to the radius between the brass points 90 and 90 of the line of sines.

### EX. III. TO FIND THE TANGENT OF 30°.

Extend the compasses from 30 to 30 on the lines of tangents, and the distance will be the tangent of 30° to the radius between the brass points 45 and 45 of the line of tangents.

### TO FIND THE COSINE OF ANY NUMBER OF DEGREES.

Most sectors have no lines of cosines; but since the cosine of any angle is the sine of the complement of that angle, therefore when the measure of an angle is given, subtract the number of degrees from 90°, and the remainder is the complement: find the sine of the number of

P 2

degrees in the remainder, and this sine is the co-sine of the number of degrees required.

EX. FIND THE COSINE OF 32°.

Having set the sector to the given radius, sub-tract 32° from 90, and the remainder is 58°.  Ex-tend the compasses from 58 to 58 on the lines of sines, and the distance is the cosine of 32° to the radius between the brass points at 90, 90.

FROM ANY GIVEN POINT, IN AN ISOMETRICAL LINE, TO DRAW AN IN-ISOMETRICAL LINE, SO AS TO REPRESENT ANY GIVEN HORIZONTAL ANGLE, AND ANY REQUIRED LENGTH,

Set the sector to the required length as a given radius, and find the cosine and sine of the given angle to this radius.   Upon the given isometrical line, and from the given point, set the sectorial radius and cosine upon the one side or the other of the given point, accordingly as the angle is required to be on one side or the other of the said point.   From the extremity of the cosine draw an isometrical line, to represent a perpen-dicular with the given isometrical line.   Upon this line, representing the perpendicular, set the sine from the extremity of the cosine.   Join the given point and the point at the unconnected ex-tremity of the sine, and the line thus drawn will be the in-isometrical line required.

### EXAMPLE.

Draw an in-isometrical line to represent a distance of 2·68 chains, and to form, at a given point, C, Plate XXX., Fig. 4, with a given isometrical line A B, an angle, which shall be the representation of a horizontal angle of 35°.

Let $a\ b\ c\ d$ be the isometrical representation of a horizontal square, the side $a\ b$ being parallel to AB, and consequently the sides $a\ d$ and $b\ c$ will represent a perpendicular to $a\ b$ or A B.

From the scale of the isometrical plan, take 2·68 chains, and set the sector to this distance as a radius. Upon A B make C E equal to the radius, and C D equal to the sectional cosine of the angle. Draw D F parallel to $a\ d$ or $b\ c$, and make D F equal to the sectional sine of this angle. Join C F by a line, which will then represent a length equal to 2·68 chains, and will form an angle with A B at C, representing a horizontal angle of 35°.

It has thus been shown that all lines, whether of geological strata, gardens, buildings, or machinery, which are either upright or parallel in square directions, forming vertical and horizontal isometrical lines, can be correctly delineated and measured by a common scale, in the most simple

P 3

and rapid manner, by simply inscribing a hexagon, in order to obtain the isometrical directions. The drawing of in-isometrical lines is somewhat more difficult, but may be readily accomplished, 1st, by geometrical construction ; 2nd, by an isometrical protractor; 3rd, by the projecting rulers ; and 4th, by the use of the sector, or by obtaining the results of sectorial operations at once from mathematical tables.

In drawing arches, or other curved or irregular lines, on an in-isometrical plane, an artist will readily discover many methods of lessening the apparent difficulties of each particular case, by the construction of ellipses, or by simple geometrical construction.   Thus, suppose that it is required to represent a circular arch of 66 feet diameter, over the in-isometrical line CF, Fig. 4, Plate XXX., the centre of which arch shall be represented by the point G,

On the isometrical line AB, the distance CE represents 2·68 chains, which is the length of the in-isometrical line CF.   Join EF, and draw GH parallel to FE.   Set off $i k$ on the line AB, at 33 feet distance on each side of the point H ; draw $i l$, $k m$, parallel to HG ; then will the distance $l m$, on the line CF, represent a distance of 66 feet, the diameter of the arch required, and the intermediate divisions, of 10 equal parts, will represent distances of 6·6 feet.

On the same scale used for the distance C E, on the line A B, take a radius of 33 feet; describe a semicircle N, and divide the diameter *o p* into 10 equal parts; draw vertical lines from each point of division, both in the semicircle N, and from the line *l m* transfer the respective heights of the arch from the vertical lines at N to the correspond_ing vertical lines above *l m*, and the extremities of the lines will indicate the curve of the ellipse which represents the in-isometrical arch over the line *l m*, and which is on the in-isometrical plane over the line C F.

In the great number and variety of plans and drawings connected with the practice of civil engineering, many instances occur in which the method of isometrical drawing would be highly explanatory and useful. To the intelligent and scientific class of professional persons who exercise the various duties of that important avocation, it is unnecessary to offer many detailed considerations on a subject which they are so competent to judge of. The favourable notice of Isometrical Plans of Mines and Machinery by the Institution of Civil Engineers, and by Mr. Telford, the able and eminent president of that society, as well as by numerous other practical and well-informed men, is a sufficient proof that the merits of this mode of drawing are at least worthy of some share of that consideration which professional persons are so competent to bestow upon it. With reference to this department, I shall, therefore, briefly observe, that as the limits of this volume preclude the advantage of having illustrations on a sufficiently large scale, I have introduced one or two small plans to give a general idea of the application of isometrical drawing to bridges, harbours, cast-iron framing, and machinery; from whence it will probably appear that it may be frequently employed with advantage for the explanation of such works.

Plate XXVII. contains a plan, elevation, and section of Tanfield Arch, near Newcastle, drawn from a correct model in the possession of the author, made from actual measurement. The isometrical drawing, Fig. 4, on the same plate, combining both the ground plan and elevation, is drawn to the same scale; and such a view of any proposed bridge would often be found a very useful accompaniment to the architectural plans and elevations. The exact lines of surface over the banks can be truly represented, and whatever is known of the foundations delineated in a very clear and intelligible manner. If the plan admit, the bed of the river may also be exactly drawn by lines showing the depth or section under any given line on the surface of the water; and if these lines be tinted with colours representing clay, gravel, rock, &c., a great deal of useful information may be comprised in the compass of a moderately-sized drawing. Suppose that the opinion of an engineer is required as to the practicability of erecting a bridge over a river and valley, which he is unable personally to inspect, is it not obvious that a correct isometrical drawing of the banks and sections of the river would give more complete and condensed information than any other mode of planning? As common ground plans and sections are data for isometrical drawings, so a correct isometrical plan may comprise, in one drawing, all the data requisite for numerous horizontal plans and vertical sections; and, with a set of triangular rulers, an engineer or architect may, in a very short time, give a more clear and distinct idea of his projected bridge, quay, or other works, than could be done by three or four of the separate plans and sections generally used.

Plate XXVIII. represents a plan, elevation, and isometrical drawing of the cast-iron circular framing lately erected at Truman's Brewery, under the able direction of Mr. Robt. Davison, the engineer of that establishment; a detailed account and drawings of which are in the library of the Institution of Civil Engineers.

Plate XXIX. represents a plan and isometrical view of Seaham Harbour, as designed by Wm. Chapman, Esq., the extensive works of which are now in active progress under the immediate super-intendence of John Buddle, Esq. To avoid complexity on so small a plan, the principal objects only are represented. The faint intersecting lines may be conceived as representing a horizon-tal plane or base coinciding with the level of the sea. Upon this base the plan of the several quays, piers, &c., is first drawn, and the several heights afterwards added. The faint dotted lines indicate the manner in which the depth or bottom of the sea or harbour may be delineated, wherever the soundings are known, as at s s s s s, &c.; and in like manner, by levelling the banks, the correct line of surface can be laid down. On a large drawing, the staiths, houses, walls, and va-rious other details, may be distinctly represented, and ships and boats also delineated in exact pro-portion to the surrounding objects.

Plate XXXI. is a plan, with front and end elevations, of a new drop or spout for ship-ping coals, the invention of the late engineer, Wm. Chapman, Esq., from whose rough papers and sketches, assisted by the explanations of his brother, Edward Chapman, Esq., a model has been recently constructed by the Author, an isometrical

representation of which is given in Plate XXXII.
This example affords a clear idea how the details
of machinery, the framing of staiths, &c., may
be represented in the plan of a quay or harbour,
when the scale is sufficiently large.

Many similar examples and illustrations might
be introduced, but the preceding may be sufficient
to elucidate the general nature and advantages of
isometrical projection. In various surveys of
projected new lines of roads and railways, the
Author has had occasion to take accurate levels
of the principal streets and roads of towns, or of
adjacent railways, preparatory to determining the
best lines of direction for the intended work.
The sections thus obtained were laid down on
isometrical plans, and by drawing lines in any
direction, and at various rates of inclination, it
could at once be exactly ascertained at what depth
such lines passed under the surface of the respective sections, so that, in a few minutes, information could be gained as to the respective levels
and depths of each line, which it would require
considerable time and calculation to obtain from
ordinary plans and sections.

It has thus been endeavoured to show, that,
by certain fixed and unvarying rules, easily understood, and attainable by a very moderate share of
attention, the most complicated lines of geological

surveys, plans of land or gardens, or drawings of harbours, bridges, machinery, &c., may be delineated, so as to combine the accuracy of a plan with the force and clearness of a picture. The rules by which this effect is accomplished, are not only easy of attainment, but depend on such obvious principles, that they partake more nearly of the character of ingenious amusement than of the labour and intricacy of many similar operations of exact science. The Author has endeavoured to render these rules, and the several examples contained in the work, as clear and intelligible as the subject will admit; and from the opinion of many able scientific and practical men, he is induced to believe, that isometrical drawing requires only to be better known, to be more generally adopted for the various kinds of representation alluded to in the present work. As a means of blending instruction and amusement, it deserves some attention from those who are intrusted with the education of youth. To ladies, the Author again respectfully submits that isometrical drawing possesses some claims on their attention, by enabling them, in an easy and correct manner, to execute landscape and garden views, drawings of antiquities, and ornamental designs of various kinds. In geology and mining, it opens out a new and interesting method of correctly delineating the surface of the earth, the arrangement of the strata, and the interior workings of mines; thus forming a correct plan and pictorial representation of the whole in one drawing.    To engineers, architects, and mechanics, and to all persons connected with the arts of building and design, isometrical delineations furnish new and explanatory illustrations of the several works, whether intended for ornamental drawings, or for working details.    In short, this mode of drawing fills up the space between the picture and the plan ; between the picturesque beauty of the painter's canvass, and the formality of the designs of · the mechanical draughtsman. Combining the accuracy of the plan with the force and clearness of the picture, it is evident that it may be rendered a most valuable and explanatory addition to the plans and drawings now commonly used ; and if it does not introduce the plans and elevations of the engineer and architect actually within the sphere of the Fine Arts, it most assuredly gives to them a strong impress of pictorial beauty, which more nearly approaches to the Fine Arts than ordinary plans and sections have hitherto commonly done.    Drawing, combined with a love of art, and an attachment to ingenious and useful occupation, tends to prepare the mind for the reception of enlightened views

and generous sentiments ; a remark which applies
to every class of society, and to every occupation
in life.    Who would not gladly see the cultivation
of such pursuits gradually displacing, and finally
banishing from our isle, those vain and frivolous
amusements, those worse than mis-spent days and
years, in which the lives of many are passed,
who, by a better direction of their talents, and
more innocent employment of their time, might
be ornaments of society, instead of being unprofit-
able members of it ?  Immense sums are annually
spent in this kingdom on pursuits and amusements, of which the very least that can be said is,
that they are frivolous in their nature, and mo-
mentary in the pleasure they afford ; and amidst
all this, how small is the share of public favour and
support which falls to the lot of many useful and
meritorious labourers in works of general usefulness ?   The noble and princely benefactions
given by the British public to the infirmaries,
public hospitals, and other charities throughout
the kingdom, and the large incomes collected
by various religious societies, strongly evince that
both piety and benevolence largely flourish and
abound.    The extravagant sums expended in
public entertainment also evince that parsimony
forms no general or widely-extended feature of
the character of the sons and daughters of England.

To a more general diffusion of a taste for rational
and simple amusements, and an extended knowledge of the various branches of art and science,
we must naturally look for a more liberal and enlightened patronage of those various departments
of human knowledge which are now comparatively
neglected, but on which the welfare and happi-
ness of mankind, and the permanent interests
of every civilized nation, most eminently depend.
As a means of cultivating a taste for the arts of
graphic design, combined with geometrical science, isometrical drawing will be found an interesting source of amusement, and a useful and
explanatory illustration of various subjects in
geology and mining; for the delineation of ornamental grounds; for the easy and expeditious construction of architectural designs; and for various
other purposes in the practice of civil engineering,
and in the wide and varied circle of the mechanical arts.

THE END.

PLATE I

Fig. 1.

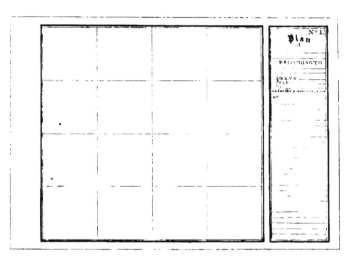

Fig. 2.

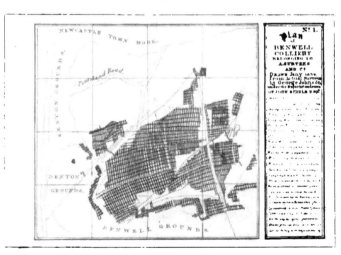

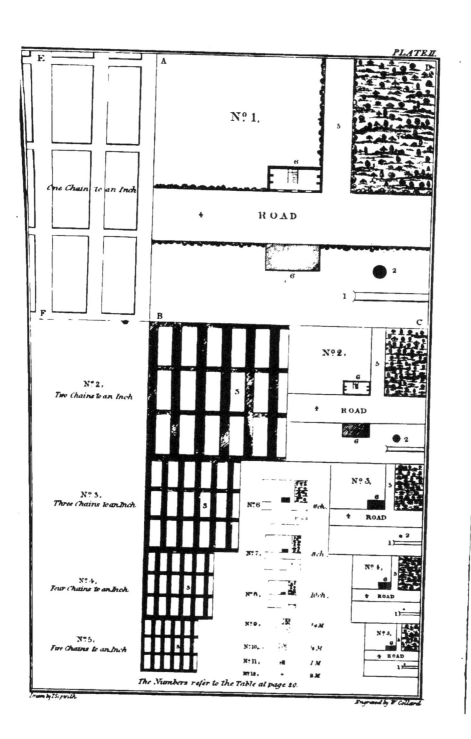

PLATE II.

The Numbers refer to the Table at page 20.

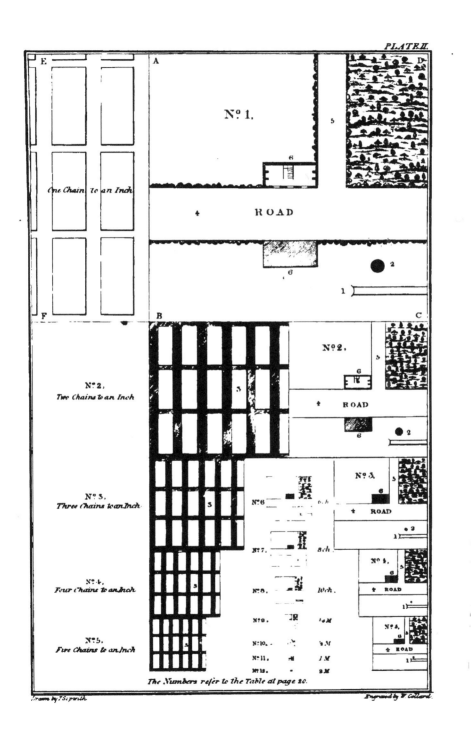

PLATE II.

E

No 1.

5

6

One Chain to an Inch

ROAD

6

2

1

A

D

B

No 2,
Two Chains to an Inch

5

No 2,

5

6

ROAD

6

2

C

No 3.
Three Chains to an Inch

5

No 6

6 ch.

No 3,

6

5

ROAD

1

2

No 7.

8 ch.

No 4,
Four Chains to an Inch

5

No 8.

10 ch.

No 4,

6

5

ROAD

1

No 5.
Five Chains to an Inch

5

No 9.

1 M

No 10.

½ M

No 5,

6

ROAD

1

No 11.

1 M

No 12.

2 M

The Numbers refer to the Table at page 20.

Drawn by T. Sipwith.                    Engraved by W. Collard.

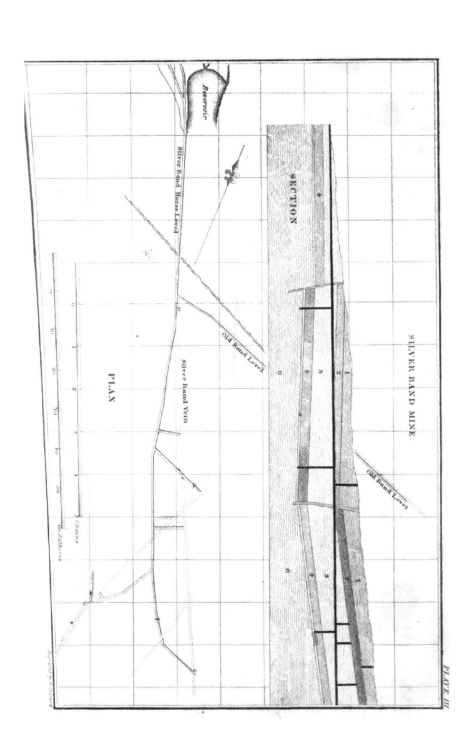

SILVER BAND MINE.

SECTION

Old Band Level

Old Band Level

Reservoir

Silver Band Horse Level

Silver Band Vein

PLAN

Chains

Fathoms

PLATE III.

PLATE II

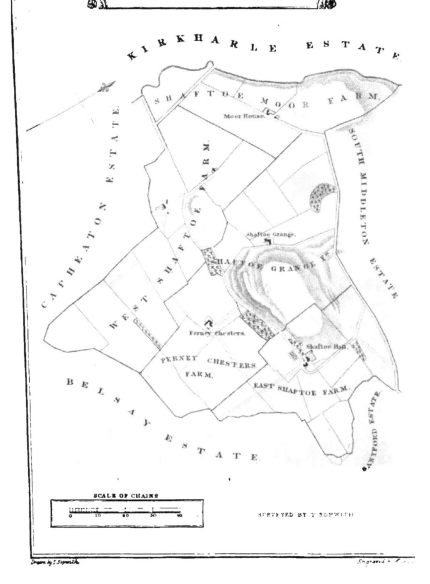

SHAFTOE ESTATE

THE PROPERTY OF THE RIGHT HONORABLE

LORD DECIES.

KIRKHARLE ESTATE

SHAFTOE MOOR FARM

Moor House.

CAPHEATON ESTATE

SHAFTOE FARM

SOUTH MIDDLETON ESTATE

Shaftoe Grange.

SHAFTOE GRANGE FARM

WEST SHAFTOE FARM

Perney Chesters.

Shaftoe Hall.

PERNEY CHESTERS FARM.

EAST SHAFTOE FARM.

BELSAY ESTATE.

ANYFORD ESTATE.

SCALE OF CHAINS

0    10    20    30    40

SURVEYED BY T SOPWITH

Drawn by T. Sopwith.                                           Engraved by R.

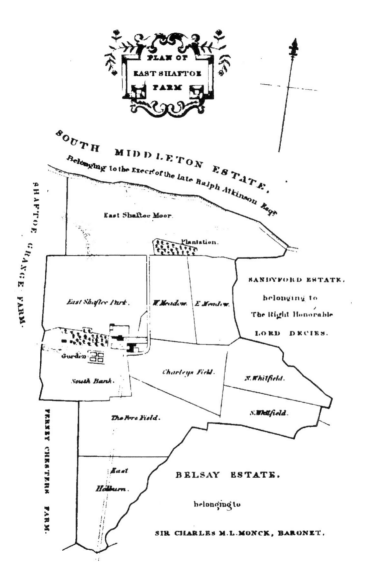

PLAN OF EAST SHAFTOE FARM

SOUTH MIDDLETON ESTATE.

Belonging to the Exec.ᵗ of the late Ralph Atkinson Esq.ʳ

SHAFTOE GRANGE FARM.

East Shaftoe Moor.

Plantation.

East Shaftoe Park.

W. Meadow. E. Meadow.

SANDYFORD ESTATE.

belonging to

The Right Honorable

LORD DECIES.

Garden.

South Bank.

Charleys Field.

N. Whitfield.

S. Whitfield.

The Fore Field.

FENBY CHESTERS FARM.

East Halburn.

BELSAY ESTATE.

belonging to

SIR CHARLES M.L. MONCK, BARONET.

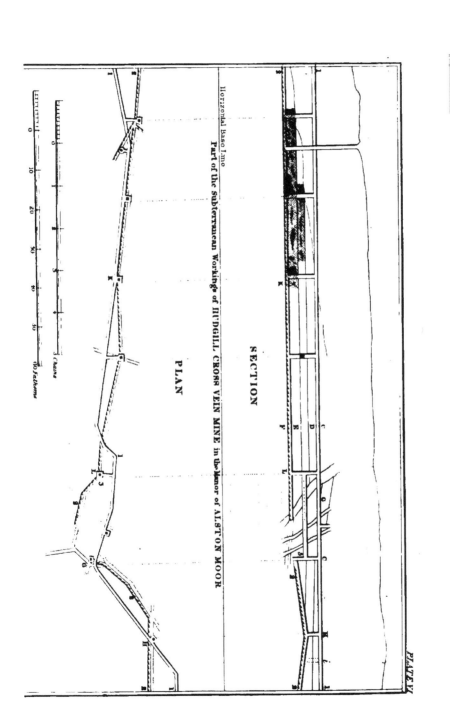

SECTION

Horizontal base line

Part of the Subterranean Workings of HUDGILL CROSS VEIN MINE in the Manor of ALSTON MOOR

PLAN

PLATE VI

PLATE VII.

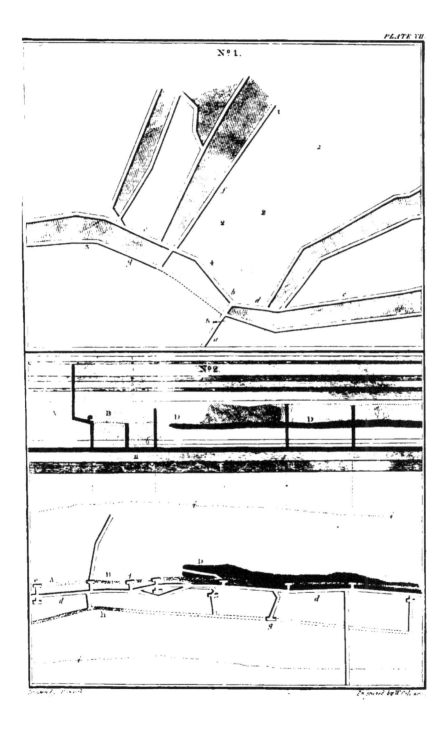

N.º 1.

N.º 2.

PLATE VI

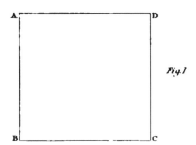

Fig.1

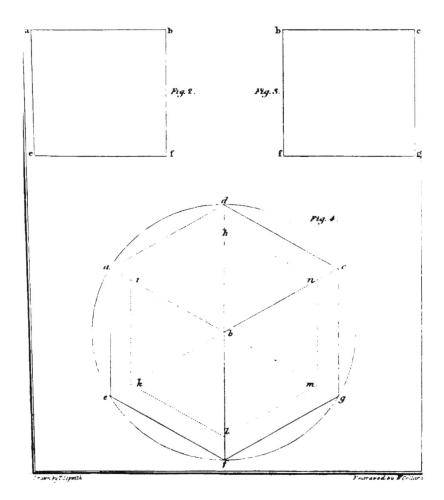

Fig. 2.

Fig.3.

Fig. 4.

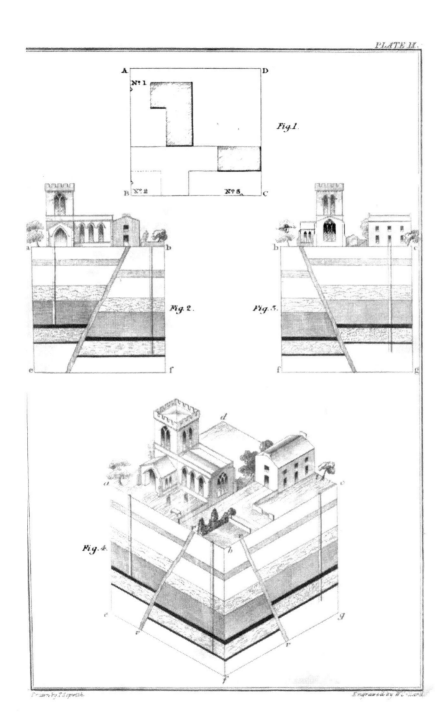

PLATE II.

Fig.1.

Fig.2.

Fig.3.

Fig.4.

PLAN OF
EAST SHAFTOE
FARM

SOUTH MIDDLETON ESTATE,
Belonging to the Execrs of the late Ralph Atkinson Esqr

SHAFTOE GRANGE FARM.

East Shaftoe Moor.

Plantation.

East Shaftoe Park.

W. Meadow.  E. Meadow.

SANDYFORD ESTATE,

belonging to

The Right Honorable

LORD DECIES.

South Bank.

Charleys Field.

N. Whitfield.

S. Whitfield.

The Fore Field.

FENJAY CHESTERS FARM.

East Holburn.

BELSAY ESTATE,

belonging to

SIR CHARLES M.L. MONCK, BARONET.

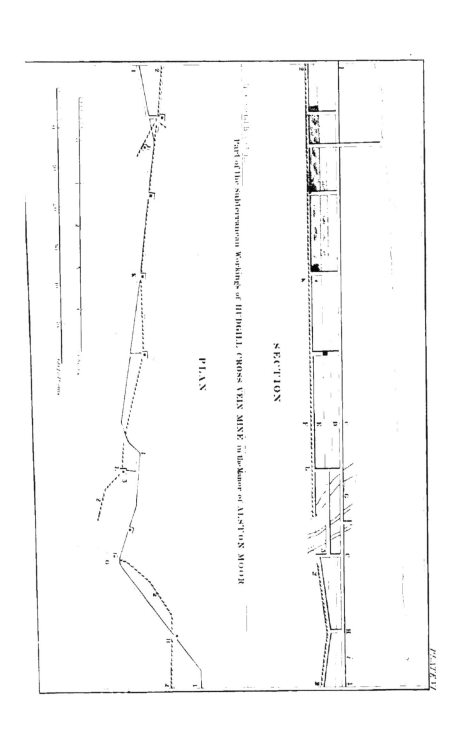

SECTION

Part of the Subterranean Workings of HUDGILL CROSS VEIN MINE in the Manor of ALSTON MOOR

PLAN

PLATE VI

PLATE VII.

Nº 1.

Nº 2

PLATE VII

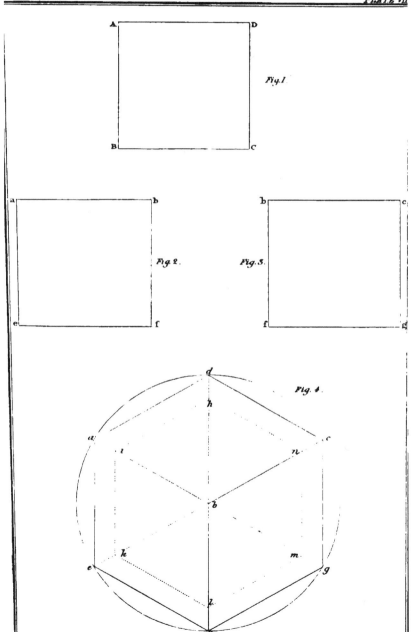

Fig. 1

Fig. 2.

Fig. 3.

Fig. 4.

PLATE II.

Fig 1.

Fig 2.

Fig 3.

Fig 4.

PLATE X.

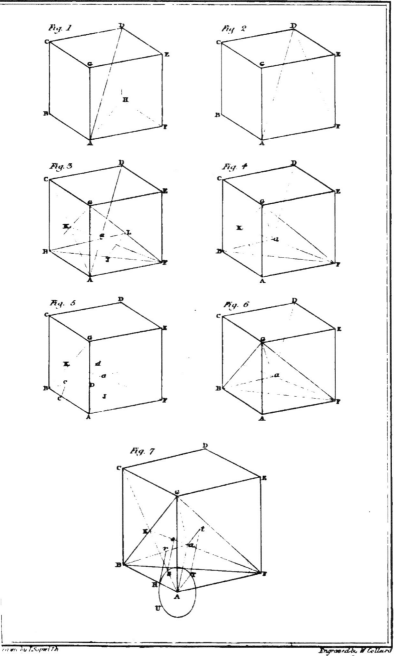

Fig. 1
Fig. 2
Fig. 3
Fig. 4
Fig. 5
Fig. 6
Fig. 7

Drawn by I. Sewel Ph.          Engraved by W Collard

PLATE XI

Fig. 1

Fig. 2

Fig. 3

LEFT HAND LINE
Right Hand Line
HORIZONTAL PLANE
Vertical Plane

RIGHT HAND LINE
Left Hand Line
HORIZONTAL PLANE
Vertical Plane

ISOMETRICAL PROTRACTORS

Fig. 4

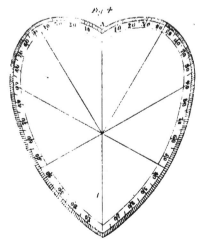

PLATE XII.

Fig. 1

Fig. 2

Scale of 4 Feet to 1 Inch

Fig. 3

Fig. 4

Fig. 5

Fig. 6

Fig. 7

Fig. 8

PLATE XIII.

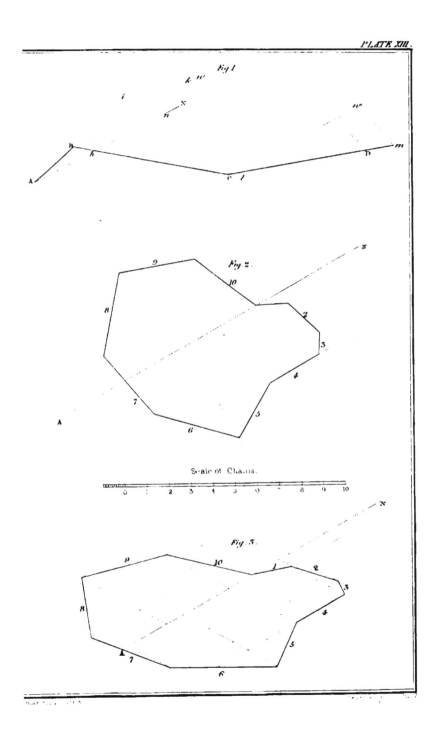

Fig 1

Fig. 2.

Scale of Chains.

Fig. 3.

PLATE XIV

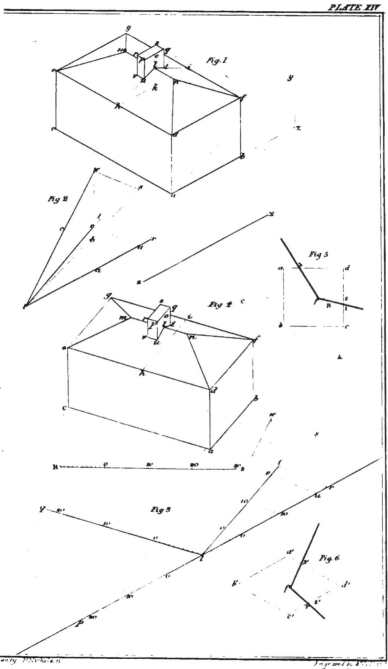

Fig. 1

Fig 2

Fig 4

Fig 5

Fig 3

Fig. 6

Genty P Nichols n.                    Ingraved b

PLATE I.

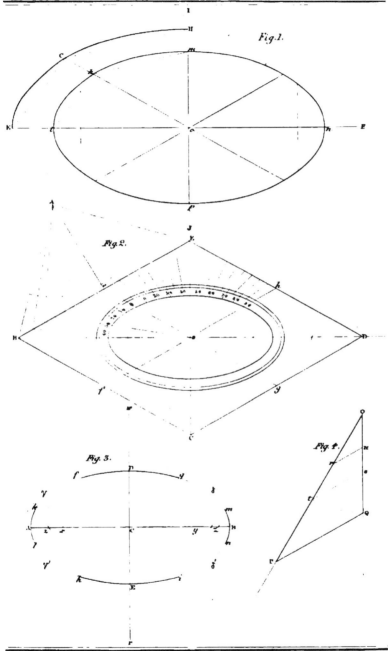

Fig.1.

Fig.2.

Fig.3.

Fig.4.

PLATE IV.

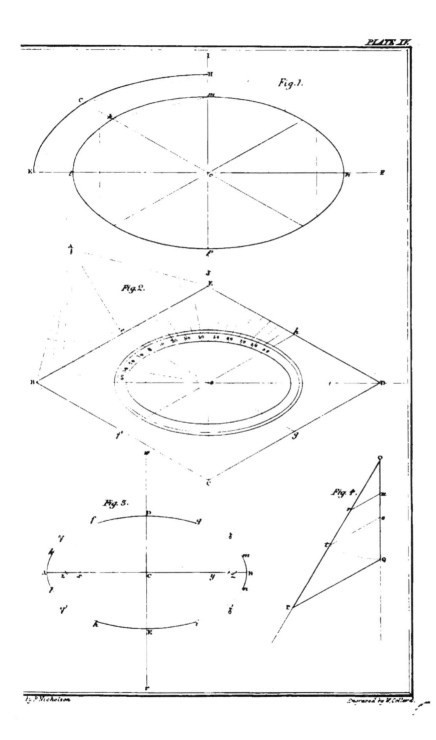

Fig. 1.

Fig. 2.

Fig. 3.

Fig. 4.

By P Nicholson

Engraved by W. Collard

PLATE IV

B

A

VERTICAL LINE

Nº 1

Isometrical Cylinder

Minor Axis

PROJECTING
AND
PARALLEL RULERS
INVENTED AND MADE BY
T. SOPWITH
Land & Mine Surveyor, 25 Royal Arcade, Newcastle

HORIZONTAL PLANE

LEFT HAND LINE HORIZONTAL PLANE

This Line to be Parallel with the under side of the paper on which the Plan or Drawing is made

Nº 2

Isometrical Projection of a Circle

1 Inch in diameter

Minor Axis

RIGHT HAND LINE HORIZONTAL PLANE

Isometrical Cube

LEFT HAND LINE HORIZONTAL PLANE

Nº 3

Isometrical Projection of a Circle

1 Inch in Diameter

Minor Axis

RIGHT HAND LINE HORIZONTAL PLANE

This Line to be parallel with the under side of the paper on which the Plan or Drawing is made

VERTICAL LINE

C

D

C

VERTICAL LINE

PROJECTING
AND
PARALLEL RULERS

INVENTED AND MADE BY

T. SOPWITH

Land & Mine Surveyor, 35 Royal Arcade, Newcastle

Nº 1

Isometrical Cylinder

Minor axis

Isometrical Cube

Nº 2

1 inch in Diameter

Isometrical projection of a circle

Minor Axis

Nº 3

1 inch in Diameter

Isometrical Projection of a Circle

Minor Axis

A

HORIZONTAL PLANE

LEFT HAND LINE HORIZONTAL PLANE

LEFT HAND LINE

RIGHT HAND LINE HORIZONTAL PLANE

HIGH HORIZONTAL PLANE

RIGHT HAND LINE HORIZONTAL PLANE

B

This Line to be Coincide with the under side of the paper on which the Plan or Drawing is made

This Line to be Parallel with the under side of the paper on which the Plan or Drawing is made

C

VERTICAL LINE

D

E

E

PLATE IV

PLATE XVII

PLATE XVIII.

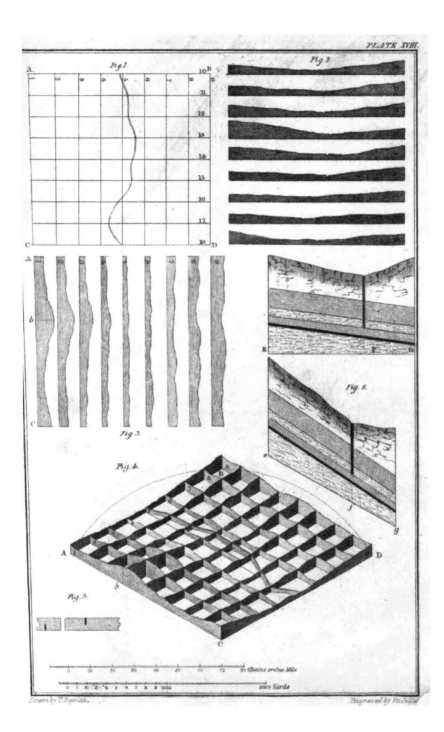

Fig. 1.

Fig. 2.

Fig. 3.

Fig. 4.

Fig. 5.

Fig. 6.

Drawn by T. Sopwith.                    Engraved by W. Collis.

PLATE XI.

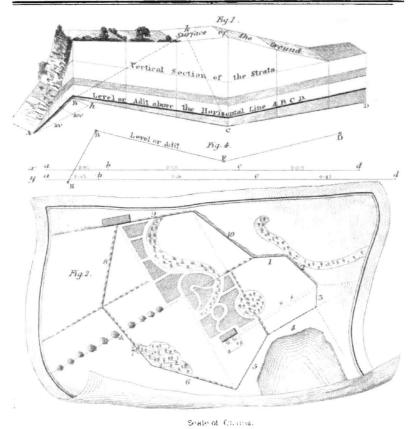

*Fig. 1.*

*Surface of the Ground*

*Vertical Section of the Strata*

*Level or Adit above the Horizontal Line A B C D.*

*Fig. 4.*

*Level or Adit*

*Fig. 2.*

Scale of Chains.

0    1    2    3    4    5    6    7    8    9    10

*Fig. 3.*

Drawn by T. Sopwith.                                          Engraved by W. ...

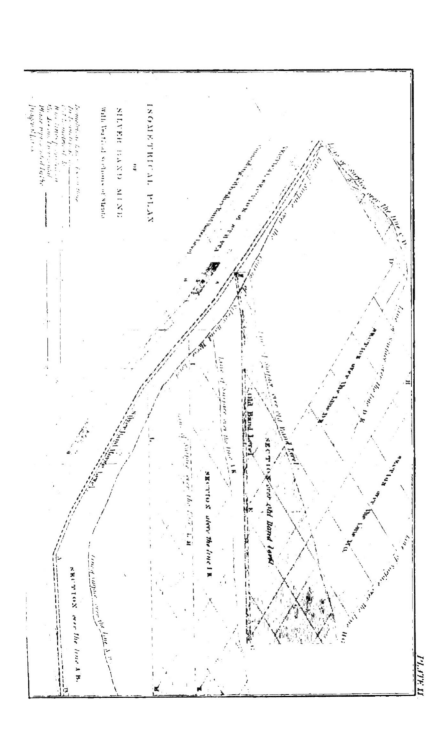

ISOMETRICAL PLAN
OF
SILVER BAND MINE
with Vertical Sections at Shafts

PLATE II.

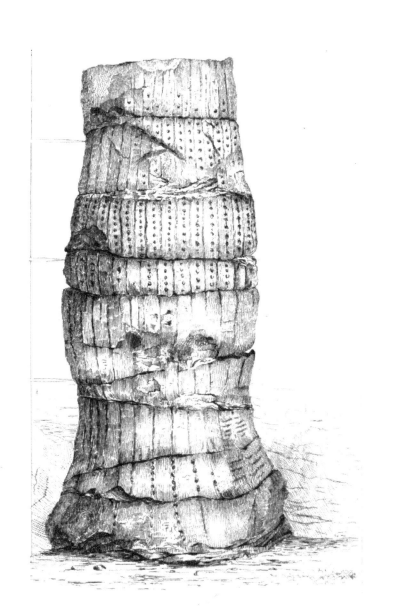

PLATE XVII.

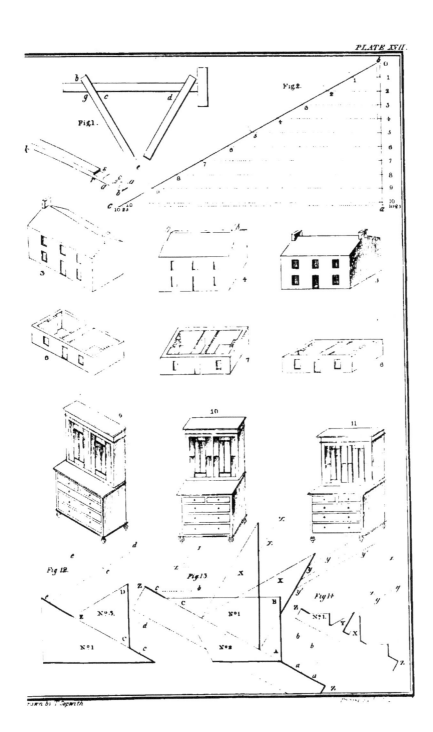

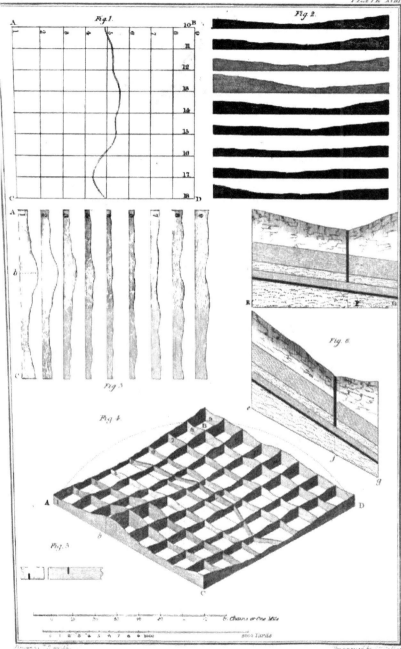

PLATE XVIII.

Fig. 1.

Fig. 2.

Fig. 3.

Fig. 6.

Fig. 4.

Fig. 5.

Chains or One Mile

Yards

PLATE XVII.

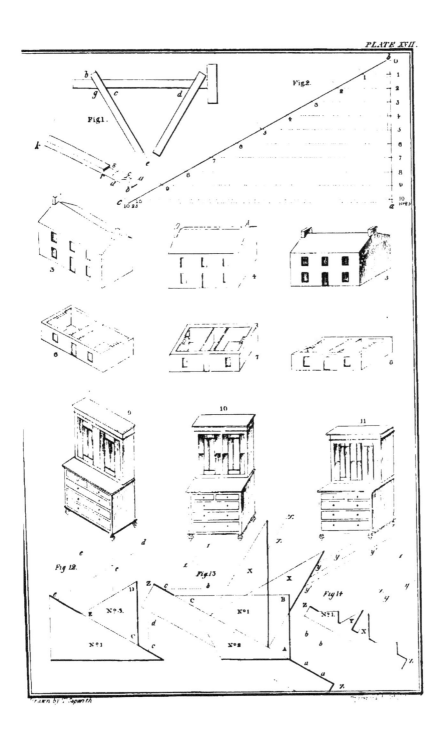

PLATE XVIII.

PLATE XVIII.

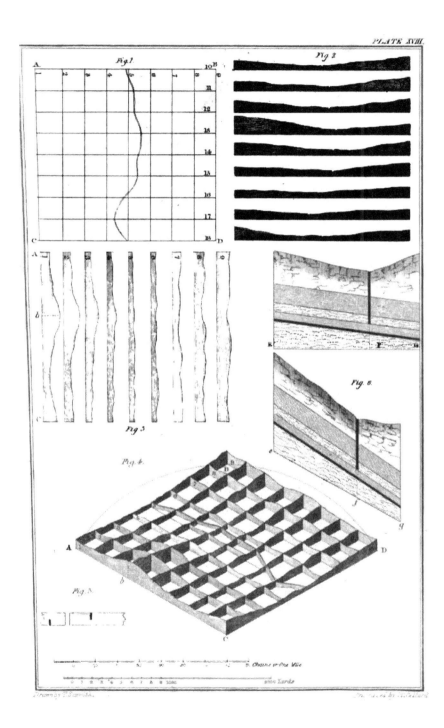

Fig. 1

Fig. 2

Fig. 3

Fig. 4

Fig. 5

Fig. 6

PLATE XI

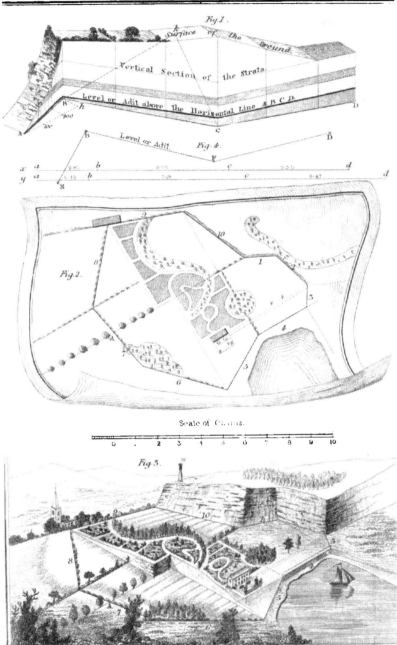

Fig. 1.

Surface of the Ground

Vertical Section of the Strata

Level or Adit above the Horizontal Line A B C D.

Level or Adit    Fig. 4.

Fig. 2.

Scale of Chains.

0    2    3    4    5    6    7    8    9    10

Fig. 3.

Drawn by T. Sopwith.                    Engraved by W.

PLATE XI

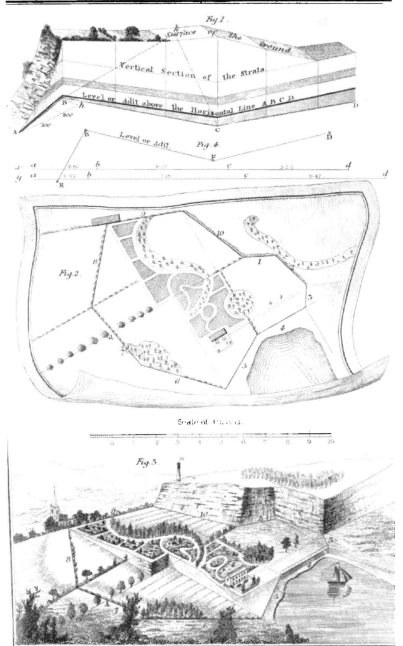

Fig. 1.

Surface of the Ground

Vertical Section of the Strata

Level or Adit above the Horizontal Line A B C D.

Fig. 4.

Level or Adit

Fig. 2.

Scale of Chains.

Fig. 3.

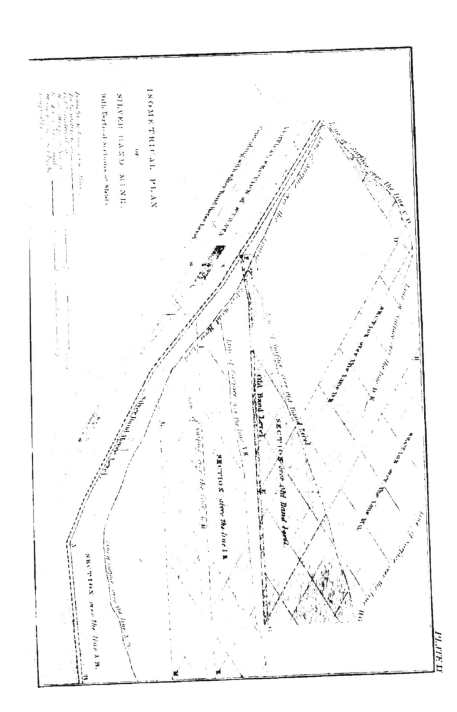

ISOMETRICAL PLAN

OF

SILVER BAND MINE.

With Vertical Sections of Shaft.

PLATE IV.

PLATE XLI.

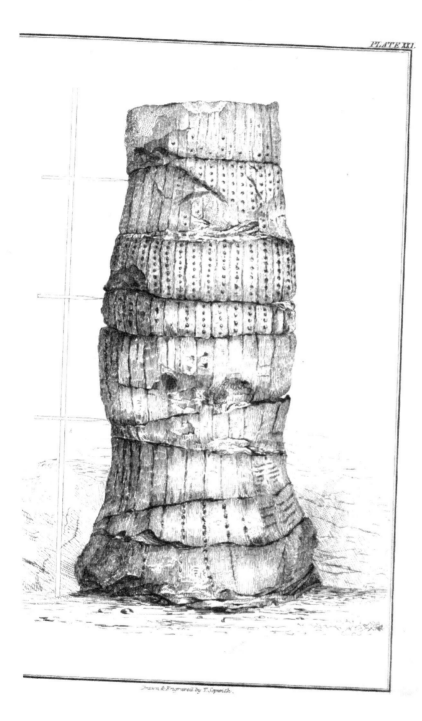

Drawn & Engraved by T. Sopwith.

PLATE XIII.

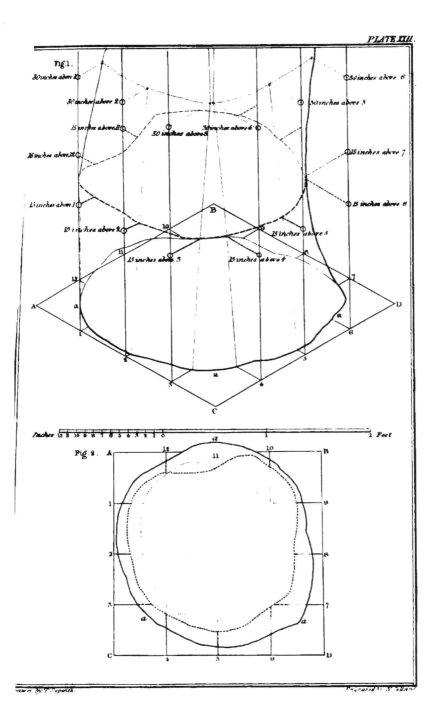

Fig.1.

30 inches above 10

30 inches above 2

15 inches above B

15 inches above 12

15 inches above 1

15 inches above 9

15 inches above 3

B

50 inches above 5    30 inches above 6

30 inches above 6

30 inches above 3

15 inches above 7

15 inches above 8

15 inches above 5

15 inches above 4

A

B

C

D

Inches 12 11 10 9 8 7 6 5 4 3 2 1 0        1        2 Feet

Fig. 2.    A        12        11        10        B

1        9

2        8

3        7

a        a

a        a

C        D

PLATE XXIII

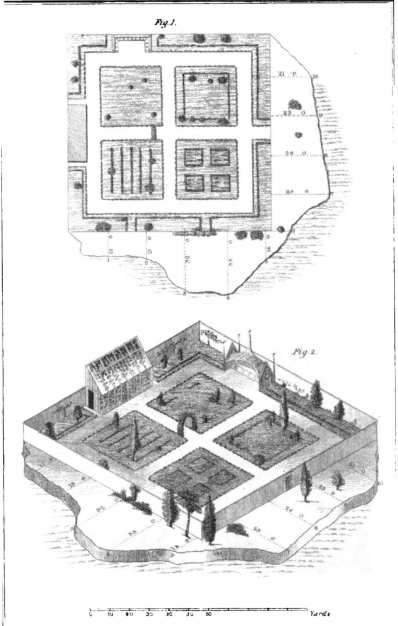

*Fig.1.*

*Fig.2.*

Yards

Drawn by T. Sopwith

Engraved by W. Collard

PLATE XXIV

Fig. 1.

Fig. 2

*PLATE XXI.*

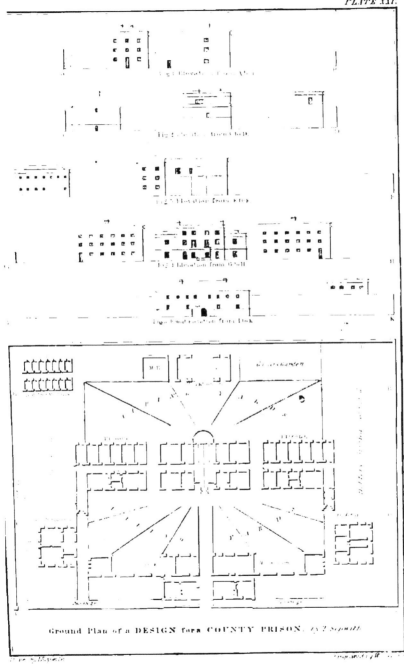

Ground Plan of a DESIGN for a COUNTY PRISON.

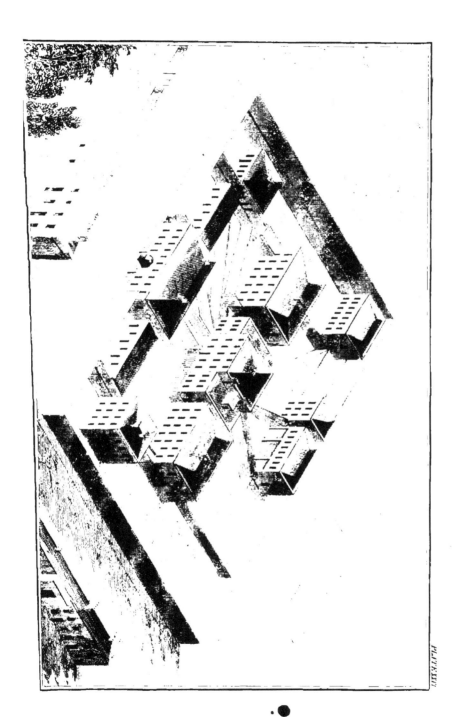

PLATE LXXXIII

PLATE XXVII.

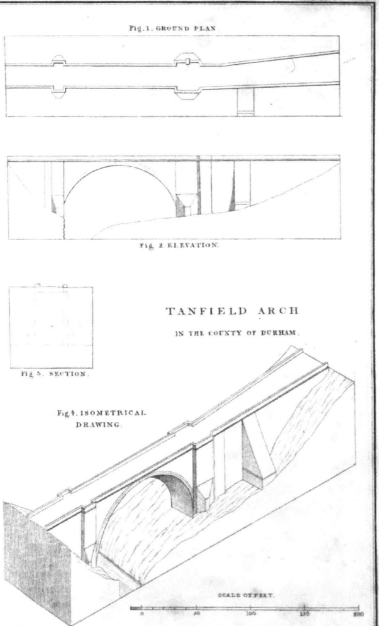

Fig.1. GROUND PLAN

Fig. 2. ELEVATION.

Fig 3. SECTION.

Fig 4. ISOMETRICAL
DRAWING.

TANFIELD ARCH

IN THE COUNTY OF DURHAM.

SCALE OF FEET.

0          50          100          150          200

Drawn by Edgworth.

Engraved by W Collie.

PLATE XII

Fig. 1.

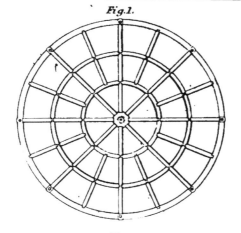

Fig. 2.

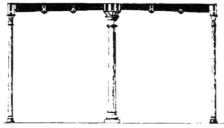

Fig 3.

Scale

Feet

DAVISON'S CIRCULAR FRAMING.

Drawn by R.Davison.                    Engraved by W. ....

PLATE XXVIII.

*Fig. 1.*

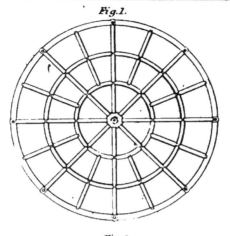

*Fig. 2.*

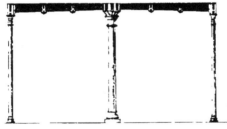

*Fig. 3.*

Scale.

20 Feet

DAVISON'S CIRCULAR FRAMING.

*PLATE XXIX.*

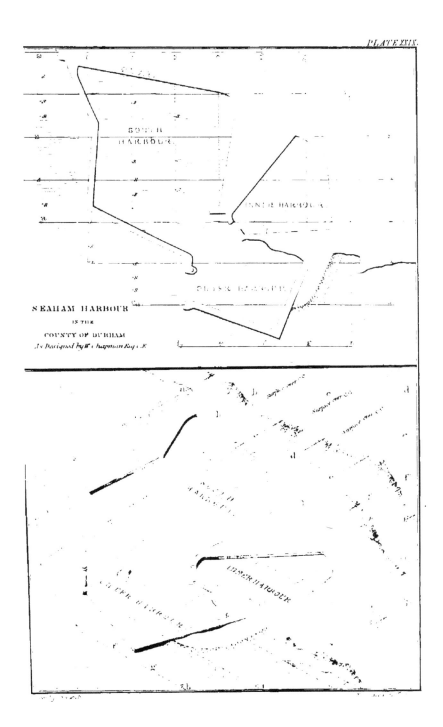

SEAHAM HARBOUR
IN THE
COUNTY OF DURHAM
As Designed by W. Chapman Esq. C.E.

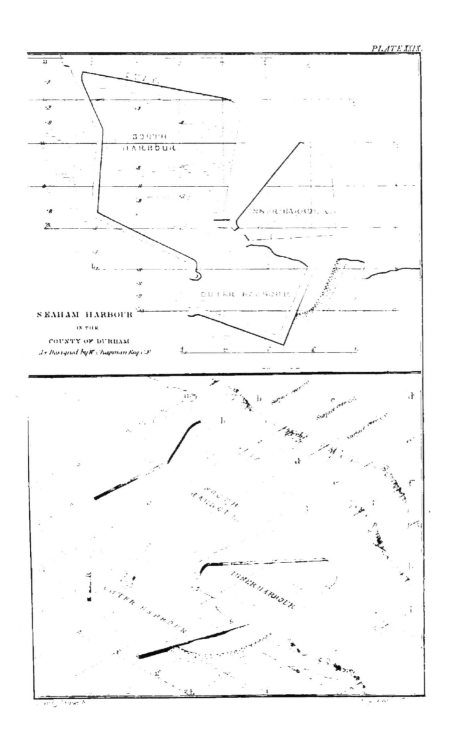

PLATE LXIX.

SEAHAM HARBOUR

IN THE

COUNTY OF DURHAM

As Designed by W. Chapman Esqr. C.E.

*PLATE XI*

*Fig 1.*

*Fig. 2.*

*Fig 3*

*Fig 4*

Drawn by T. Sopwith.

Engraved by W. Coats

PLATE XX.

Fig.1.    Fig.2.

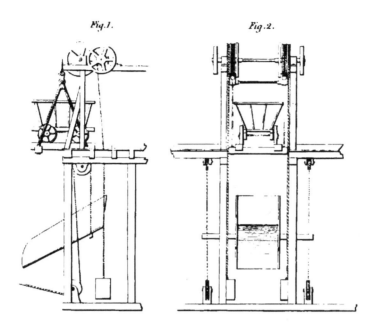

Fig.3.

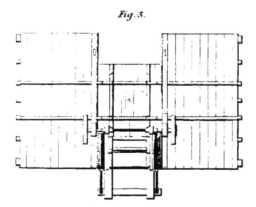

PLATE XXXI

Fig. 1.  Fig. 2.

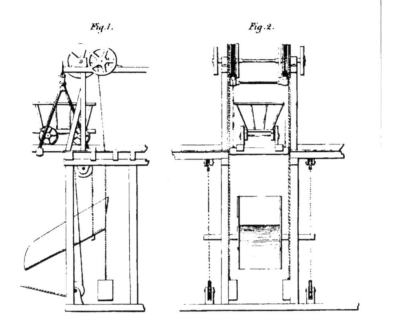

Fig. 3.

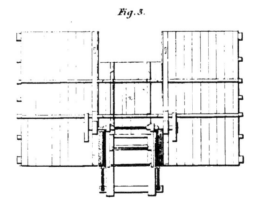

PLATE. XXVI

# TAYLOR'S
# ARCHITECTURAL LIBRARY,
## 59, HIGH HOLBORN, LONDON.

## JOHN WEALE,

*(Of the late Firm of Priestley and Weale, High Street, Bloomsbury.)*

BEGS to announce his Removal to, and purchase of, the
above Establishment, so long and eminently conducted by
the late Mr. JOSIAH TAYLOR, and at which will be found
all Works on ARCHITECTURE and BUILDING, GREEK, ROMAN,
ITALIAN, LOUIS 14th, GOTHIC, of various Eras, CASTELLATED,
ELIZABETHAN, and FLEMISH. COTTAGE and VILLA and RU-
RAL ARCHITECTURE. ORNAMENTS and DECORATIONS, GREEK,
ROMAN, CINQUE CENTO, ARABESQUE, LOUIS 14th, and OLD
ENGLISH. CABINET FURNITURE and UPHOLSTERY, of the
newest Fashions and interior Decorations. ENGINEERING,
BRIDGES, HARBOURS, DOCKS, CANALS, RAIL-ROADS, STEAM
ENGINES, &c. &c. &c. rendering this House the fixed Mart
for the Architect, Builder, Engineer, Student, and Amateur.

PUBLISHED THIS DAY,

## BY JOHN WEALE.

A TREATISE ON ISOMETRICAL DRAWING, as
applicable to Geological and Mining Plans, Picturesque
Delineations of Ornamental Grounds, Perspective Views
and Working Plans of Buildings and Machinery, and to
general Purposes of Civil Engineering; with Details of improved Methods of preserving Plans and Records of Subterranean Operations in Mining Districts. With Thirty-four
Copperplate Engravings. By T. SOPWITH, Land and Mine
Surveyor; Member of the Institution of Civil Engineers;
Author of "Geological Sections of Mines;" "Account of
Mining Districts," &c.

"Isometrical perspective is preferable to common perspective on
many accounts; it is much easier and simpler in its principles; it is

A

also incomparably more easy and accurate in its application. The information given by isometrical drawings is much more definite and precise than that obtained by the usual methods, and better fitted to direct a workman in execution."—PROFESSOR FARISH.

" Isometrical views of building ought to be in universal use among architects. The elevation which this mode of drawing produces, is highly explanatory and expressive."—J. C. LOUDON.

ALSO, RECENTLY PUBLISHED,

**GEOLOGICAL SECTIONS OF HOLYFIELD, HUDGILL CROSS VEIN AND SILVER-BAND LEAD MINES, IN ALSTON MOOR AND TEES-DALE**; showing the various Strata and Subterranean Operations. Engraved on three Copper-plates, 24 inches by 12 inches; 17 inches by 7 inches, and 20 inches by 10 inches, and coloured, with Letter-press Description, &c. By T. SOPWITH. Price 10s. 6d.

These plans exhibit the subterraneous workings of the mines, by a horizontal or ground plan, and by an upright or vertical section : the former exhibits the course and bearing of the veins, and the levels, cross-cuts, drifts, &c., by which access is had to the veins for procuring lead ore. The section shows the order of superposition, and various thickness of the strata as they occur in different mining fields, with the workings in them. Such data, by supplying numerous records of established facts in the disposition and changes of the strata, the position of veins, and their productiveness under various circumstances, must be of essential service in a study where a knowledge of facts and a patient investigation of practical results, are the only sources from which any important discoveries can be derived.

**HISTORICAL AND DESCRIPTIVE ACCOUNT OF ALL SAINTS' CHURCH, in Newcastle upon Tyne**, illustrated with Plans, Views, and Architectural Details, including an Account of the Monuments, with Armorial Bearings, &c. By T. SOPWITH. Demy octavo. Eleven Engravings. Price 10s. 6d.

The present church of All Saints is the most splendid architectural ornament which modern times have produced in Newcastle, being equally conspicuous for the novelty and convenience of its plan, as for the variety of its decorations. In attempting to compile an accurate and detailed account of this, and the former structure, the writer has carefully selected the most valuable information, and availed himself of opportunities of procuring materials from original and authentic sources. The antiquity and numerous endowments of the old, and the many interesting circumstances connected with the erection of the new church, are subjects which are not devoid of interest to the inhabitants of a town of which it is so distinguished an ornament, and still less to the parishioners who have reared so fair a monument of their munificence and taste.

This work being chiefly of local interest, nearly the whole impression has been sold in Newcastle, and a few copies only remain.

**EIGHT VIEWS OF FOUNTAINS ABBEY, in-**

tended to illustrate the Architectural and Picturesque Beauties of that celebrated Ruin. Engraved on Copper-plate, from original Drawings by J. Metcalf and J. W. Carmichael. With an HISTORICAL and ARCHITECTURAL DESCRIPTION. By T. SOPWITH. Dedicated, by Permission, to Mrs. Lawrence, Studley Park. The following are the subjects represented in the views :—I. East View of the Abbey. II. Interior of the Lady Chapel. III. Interior of the Church. IV. East Window, &c., from the Interior. V. Chapter House, from the Cloister Garden. VI. Interior of the Refectory. VII. The Hospitium. VIII. West View of the Abbey. Royal Folio, Price 10s. 6d.

· " The sketch conveys all the general idea of Fountains that tourist or antiquary can wish, detailed with truth, spirit, and feeling."—Letter from R. SURTEES, of Mainsforth, Esq., Author of the History of Durham.

AN ACCOUNT OF THE MINING DISTRICTS OF ALSTON MOOR, WEARDALE, AND TEESDALE, IN CUMBERLAND AND DURHAM; comprising descriptive Sketches of the Scenery, Antiquities, Geology, and Mining Operations in the Upper Dales of the Rivers Tyne, Wear, and Tees. By T. SOPWITH.

" The practical operation of mining itself, with a comparison of the ancient and modern modes, and some hints as to the ways and means of a miner's existence, lead us to the chapter headed " *A Visit to a Lead Mine*," the whole of which we would extract if our space would permit, but we must content ourselves with remarking that the circumstances of many mines are here crowded into one picture, and grouped with such effect, that we see and feel as we read. Yadmoss, Cauldron Snout, the High Fence, Barnard-castle, and the Dale scenery are admirably described."—*Atlas, June 23*, 1833.

PLAN OF THE MINING DISTRICT OF ALSTON MOOR, with Part of the Dales of Tyne, Wear, and Tees, and the several New Lines of Road recently made in these Districts. By T. SOPWITH. Price 1s. 6d., plain; 2s. 6d. coloured.

PLAN OF THE VALE OF DERWENT, near Newcastle, showing the new Line of Road, with a Letter-press Description, &c. By T. SOPWITH. Price 7s. 6d.

A SET OF PROJECTING AND PARALLEL RULERS, invented by T. SOPWITH, for constructing Working Plans and Drawings in Isometrical and other Modes of Projection, may be had of the Booksellers. Price 2s. 6d.

A TREATISE ON DIALLING, comprising the Delineation of Sun Dials, in every Position to the Plane of the Horizon, in two Parts, independent of each other; the one showing the Geometrical, and the other the Arithmetical Construction, which are reduced to the greatest degree of simplicity by the adoption of a new Plan, consisting of fewer and more uniform Precepts than have hitherto been accomplished; with a New Method of Drawing a Meridian Line, and the Application of the Formula derived from the Trahedral, to the Angles of the Faces and Edges of Pyramids, the regular Solids and Roofs. By Peter Nicholson, Architect, Author of The Carpenter's New Guide, The Principles of Architecture, The Builder's Director, A Practical Treatise on Masonry and Stone Cutting, &c. &c., as also of several Mathematical Works : Honorary Member of the Literary and Philosophical Society ; and of the Literary, Scientific, and Mechanical Institution of Newcastle upon Tyne.

### PREPARING FOR PUBLICATION.

A GENERAL TREATISE ON PROJECTION, showing the various Modes of Delineating Lines, Plane Figures, and Solids, so as to present, upon immediate inspection, a striking image of the object to be carried into execution ; as also showing the Methods of Measuring the Lineal Parts by Scales, and exhibiting the Projections of the Intersections of Square and Round Bodies with one another. By Peter Nicholson, Author of the Carpenter's Guide, the Builder's Director, the Principles of Architecture, &c.

### ELIZABETHAN ARCHITECTURE.

DOMESTIC ARCHITECTURE. The History and Description of the Architecture, Construction, Materials, &c. of Eastbury, Essex, with plans of each floor, sections, elevations, details and views, also copies of the fresco paintings ; in 16 plates, imperial 4to., £2 2s. plain ; and £3 3s. on India paper ; drawn and engraved by and under the superintendence of T. H. Clarke, Architect.

This building being one of the finest specimens of the Domestic Architecture of this country, executed about the time of Edward the VI., and being fully illustrated, it is presumed, cannot fail to be of great practical use both to the Architect and Builder, and wanted as an example of a style now much followed in the erection of noblemen's and gentlemen's houses.

A SERIES OF VIEWS OF ENGLISH MANSIONS, Palaces, Halls, &c., erected in the reigns of Queen Elizabeth and James the First, several of which no longer exist. Twenty Drawings on Stone, with description, imperial 8vo., cloth boards, price One Guinea.

DETAILS OF ELIZABETHAN ARCHITECTURE, by H. SHAW, F.S.A. 2 Numbers, containing 10 plates, 10s., 4to.

ANCIENT FURNITURE, by H. SHAW, F.S.A. 7 Numbers, 4to., 35 plates, 35s.

HISTORY AND ARCHITECTURE OF HATFIELD HOUSE. (The Marquis of Salisbury's.) Atlas folio, very fine plates of plans, elevations, sections, and views, £3: 3s. A fine specimen of this period.

HISTORY AND ARCHITECTURE OF HARD-WICKE HALL, in Derbyshire (the Duke of Devonshire's). Atlas folio, very fine plates of plans, elevations, sections, views, interior views; shewing the furniture and fittings.— A beautiful work of this admired style will be published on October 1st, subscribers' names previously received by Mr. WEALE, and specimen plates to be seen.

MR. JOHN TURNER'S large folio plate of the SCREEN in Middle Temple Hall, drawn from actual measurement, very neatly etched, price 6s.

### ENGINEERING AND MECHANICS.

A new edition, just received from America, of OLIVER EVANS ON MILL WORK; much improved and amplified by T. P. JONES, 8vo., 25 Plates, price 18s.

THE CIVIL ENGINEER AND MACHINIST. DIVISION 1.—Atlas folio, containing BOULTON and WATT'S STEAM ENGINE, with detailed Plates one-fourth of the full size, price £1 1s. DIVISION 2,—To be published August 20th, comprising MARINE ENGINES and CORN MILLS, price £1 1s. Subscribers have earliest copies by application to Mr. WEALE.

MECHANICS FOR PRACTICAL MEN;—containing explanations of the principles of Mechanics; the Steam Engine, with its various proportions; Parallel Motion, and Tables of Safety-Valve Levers, &c.; Tables of the weight of Cast Iron Pipes; Tables of various kinds, on cast and wrought Iron, for the use of Founders, Smiths, &c.; strength and stress of Materials, &c.; Hydrostatics and Hydraulics; dissertation on Rail-roads, &c. &c. By J. HANN and ISAAC DODDS, Civil Engineers, Plates, 8vo., price 7s. 6d.

PRACTICAL VIEW OF THE STEAM ENGINE; illustrated by elephant folio engravings of the largest Machine in Scotland, constructed by Messrs. C. Girdwood and Co., for the Coal Mines of Sir John Hope, of Craighall, Bart., with an account of a Mercurial Statical Dynamometer, and results of the draught of Horses, quantum of friction on Railway, &c. By I. MILNE. Letter-press description in

8vo., with 2 Plates to accompany the 2 large elephant folio plates, £1 1s.

A TREATISE ON THE PRINCIPAL MATHE-MATICAL INSTRUMENTS employed in Surveying, Levelling, and Astronomy. By F. W. SIMMS. Wood-cuts, 8vo., 5s.

AN ESSAY ON THE CONSTRUCTION OF THE FIVE ARCHITECTURAL SECTIONS OF CAST IRON BEAMS employed as Girders, Bressummers, and other Horizontal supports for Buildings, &c. &c. By WILLIAM TURNBULL, wood-cuts, 8vo., 4s. 6d.

COMPLETE ASSISTANT for the Landed Proprietor, Estate and House Agent, Land Steward, Proctor, Architect, &c. 8vo., 16s.

COCKBURN'S (Major) ANTIQUITIES OF POM-PEII, a splendid Work in 2 large folio vols., very fine Plates, engraved by WILLIAM COOKE, and the text written by T. L. DONALDSON, Esq., Architect. £8 8s. (published at £21).

## ORNAMENTS.—VARIOUS.

CHIPPENDALE'S ONE HUNDRED AND THIR-TY-THREE DESIGNS OF INTERIOR DECORA-TIONS IN THE OLD FRENCH STYLES, for Carvers, Cabinet Makers, Ornamental Painters, Brass Workers, Modellers, Chasers, Silversmiths, general Designers, and Architects; 50 Plates quarto, consisting of Hall, Glass, and Picture Frames, Chimney Pieces, Stands for China, &c., Clock and Watch Cases, Girandoles, Brackets, Grates, Lanterns, Ornamental Furniture, and Cielings; royal 4to., price £1 1s. neatly bound.

CHIPPENDALE'S DESIGNS for Sconces, Chimney and Looking Glass Frames, in the old French style, adapted for Carvers and Gilders, fashionable and ornamental Cabinet Makers, Modellers, &c. 11 Plates, 4to., price 7s.

A BOOK OF ORNAMENTS in the French and antique styles. By T. JOHNSON, Carver, 8 Plates, 12mo., price 3s. 6d.

DESIGNS FOR VASES, on 17 Plates, 12mo,, 4s. 6d.

SPECIMENS OF THE CELEBRATED ORNA-MENTS AND INTERIOR DECORATIONS OF THE AGE OF LOUIS XIV., selected from the magnificent work of Meissonnier. 4to., 15 Plates, 9s.

DARLY'S BOOK OF ORNAMENTS, 7 Plates, large oblong 4to., 1s. 6d.

ORNAMENTS IN THE ANTIQUE TASTE, 6 Plates, 4to., 1s. 6d.

DESIGNS OF THE ORNAMENTS AND DECO-RATIONS OF CHIMNEY PIECES of the middle of the last century, 20 Plates, in 4to., Price 6s.

DESIGNS OF DOORS AND WINDOWS, in the Italian and Palladian styles, 10 Alates, 8vo., 4s.

HOUSEHOLD FURNITURE, in the taste of a century ago, containing upwards of 350 designs on 120 Plates, large 8vo., 7s.

A BOOK OF ORNAMENTS, drawn and engraved by M. Lock, principally adapted for Carvers, but generally useful for various Decorations in the old French taste, six Plates, Octavo, stitched, price 3s.

A BOOK OF ORNAMENTS, suitable for Beginners, by Thomas Pether, Carver, 5 Plates, oblong, price 1s. 6d.

DESIGNS FOR CHIMNEY PIECES, AND CHIMNEY GLASSES the one above the other, in the times of Inigo Jones, and Sir John Vanbrugh. 10 Plates, 8vo., price 4s.

### GOTHIC ARCHITECTURE.

THE ANTIQUITIES OF THE PRIORY OF CHRIST CHURCH, Hants. Consisting of Plans, Elevations, Sections, Details, and Perspective Views; accompanied by Historical and Architectural Accounts of the Priory Church, together with some general particulars of the Castle and Borough. By Benjamin Ferrey, Architect; the Literary Part by E. W. Brayley, Esq. 4to., 18 beautiful Engravings, price 2l. 5s., and on large paper 3l. 7s. 6d.

THE ANCIENT GATES AND FORTIFICATIONS OF THE CITY OF YORK, illustrated by a series of etchings from original drawings. By H. F. Lockwood and A. H. Cates, Architects. 4to., 18s.; large paper, India, 30s.

MOORE'S LIST OF THE PRINCIPAL CASTLES AND MONASTERIES IN GREAT BRITAIN. 8vo., 3s., (published at 7s.)

PUGIN'S SECOND SERIES OF EXAMPLES OF GOTHIC ARCHITECTURE. The 2 vols. now complete; vol. 2 to be had separately, each vol. 4l. 4s., containing numerous plates.

PUGIN'S SPECIMENS OF GOTHIC ARCHITECTURE, 2 vols., numerous plates; in 4to., 6l. 6s.; on large paper, 9l. 9s.

ATTICA.—THE UNEDITED ANTIQUITIES OF ATTICA. By the Society of Dilettanti. Royal folio, with 78 very fine plates, 3l. 3s., in cloth boards, and lettered.

SUGGESTIONS FOR THE ARCHITECTURAL IMPROVEMENT OF THE WESTERN PART OF LONDON. By SYDNEY SMIRKE, F.S.A., F.G.S. Plates, imperial 8vo., extra bound, 7s.

REPORTS, ESTIMATES, AND TREATISES ON CANALS, RIVERS, HARBOURS, PIERS, BRIDGES, DRAINING, EMBANKING, LIGHT-HOUSES, MACHINERY, FIRE ENGINES, MILLS, &c. By J. SMEATON, Civil Engineer. 3 vols., 4to., 74 plates, boards, £4 14s. 6d. Published at £7 7s.

LETTERS OF AN ARCHITECT, FROM FRANCE, ITALY, AND GREECE. By JOSEPH WOODS, F.L.S., F.G.S., &c. In 2 vols., 4to., published at £4 4s., in boards, illustrated with twenty-one copper-plates and seventy-three wood-cuts; or with proof impressions of the copper-plates on India paper, published at £5 5s., now reduced to £2 2s.; India proofs, £2 12s. 6d.

*₊* This Work is recommended to the Professors of Architecture and to Amateurs as the only intellectual literary and scientific work on the diversified styles and beauties of Architecture found and investigated in the countries which Mr. Woods visited; the subjects of which are amply and ably criticised.

IN THE PRESS,

ELEMENTARY AND PRACTICAL INSTRUCTIONS ON THE ART OF BUILDING COTTAGES AND HOUSES FOR THE HUMBLER CLASSES. An easy method of constructing Earthen Walls, adapted to the erection of Dwelling Houses, Agricultural and other Buildings, surpassing those built of timber in comfort and stability, and equalling those built of Brick; at the same time effecting a considerable saving in the expense, as it may be performed by any person without previous experience, and in any climate: to which is added, a Practical Treatise on the Manufacture of Bricks and Lime, and on the arts of Digging Wells, and Draining, Rearing, and Managing a Vegetable Garden; of the Management of Pigs, Poultry, Sheep, and other Cattle; making of Bacon, Hams, &c., for Winter Stock. The whole applied for the use of

EMIGRANTS;

To the better Lodging of the Peasantry of Ireland, and to those districts to which the benevolence of Landed Proprietors is now directed. With six Plates of Plans and Elevations, and several Wood-cuts of Details.

J. BLACKWELL AND CO., PRINTERS, NEWCASTLE.